THINK
INDIGENOUS

THINK INDIGENOUS

NATIVE AMERICAN SPIRITUALITY
FOR A MODERN WORLD

DOUG GOOD FEATHER

Transcribed by Doug Red Hail Pineda

HAY HOUSE, INC.
Carlsbad, California • New York City
London • Sydney • New Delhi

Published in the United States by: Hay House, Inc.: www.hayhouse.com®
Published in Australia by: Hay House Australia Pty. Ltd.: www.hayhouse
.com.au • *Published in the United Kingdom by:* Hay House UK, Ltd.: www
.hayhouse.co.uk • *Published in India by:* Hay House Publishers India:
www.hayhouse.co.in

Cover design: Doug Good Feather • *Interior design:* Nick C. Welch
Credit for image on page 24: Amy Starspeaker

**Cataloging-in-Publication Data on file at
the Library of Congress**

Tradepaper ISBN: 978-1-4019-5616-5
E-book ISBN: 978-1-4019-5617-2

14 13 12 11 10 9 8 7
1st edition, April 2021

Printed in the United States of America

I wrote this story for you, but when I was writing it, I did not realize that you would be gone before it was finished and your teachings would be such a big part of my writing and life. Cassandra Ann Good Feather—Good Hearted Eagle Woman, my second eldest daughter, diagnosed with leukemia at 21 after she found out she was having a baby, my grandson Zuya Ohitika. As the illness took its usual course and took her life along with that of my grandson, she was brave and strong. Cassie truly was the kindest warrior I have ever known, and her life and sacrifice have shown me what true love really means. As your father, I am grateful that you chose me to be your dad. I want to thank you and honor your life by continuing to live a good life and sharing all that I have learned. Until I see you again.
—Your humble father

CONTENTS

PREFACE

We have arrived at this place, this spiritual way of life, together—but we took very different paths. This is, of course, true of everyone and everything in this life. We all walk our own path, but so often, we come to the very same conclusion. Perhaps you will come to this same conclusion as well.

This book is my way of life. I live these ways. I was raised in these traditional indigenous ways on the Standing Rock Indian Reservation, but, growing up all those years, I didn't have a clue what a gift that was. I think about the way I was raised . . . I was raised to be a warrior. But to be a warrior, I wasn't taught about war. I was taught about love, compassion, generosity, fortitude, and courage. All of the things I needed to know and understand in order to take care of myself and be a warrior of peace and love.

In order to be a part of a community, you have to start with yourself. People benefit from that because they don't have to take care of you—you can take care of them and become the next teacher, passing on the values and virtues that you were raised with. Self-reliance and self-love come first. That's the first stage.

But as we get older, we go through different stages of life and different rites of passage. In my community, I became a scout, or a sentinel, watching over the camp. If danger came, I was to be a protector. If I didn't have the understanding of self-love and self-reliance, I wouldn't have been able to learn to love the community, to have compassion for the people around me. I had to love myself in order to love and protect others.

Of course, I didn't always remember that. When I returned from war as a combat veteran, I was damaged. Some wounds were visible, and some were unseen. I'd been married, but my marriage became further collateral damage from that war. I had to go through my own process of healing. And my community helped heal me. I immersed myself back into our traditional ways to try and find answers, and I reconnected with my elders to help heal and call my spirit back into my body. And I realized how effective this way of life is, this way of working with and helping people. It's more of a natural and nurturing way. I realized how powerful this way of life that I took for granted really is.

Part of realizing the power of walking an indigenous spiritual way of life comes from prayer, from connecting directly with God, or the Creator. Growing up, I went to church, and my community was deeply spiritual, but it wasn't until I left the reservation that I realized I didn't know how to pray. I think a lot of us are like that. We go to church and we recite these prayers, or we listen to our elders pray, but nobody teaches us how to do it for ourselves. And when I left home, I needed to pray. Church was synthetic, and our indigenous ceremonies were organic, and I was raised with one foot in each world . . . I felt so lost.

And so I just talked to the Creator. It was all I knew how to do. I said, "I don't know how to pray, but I hope you hear me. I hope you hear my voice that I send to you as I stand here before you. I ask you to guide me on this journey as I go into the world on my own. I'm scared; I feel lost; I don't feel like I belong here, or anywhere. But I trust in you, that you will bring me to where I need to be."

That's the way I learned to pray, just talking. The more I did it, the more comfortable I felt. And my prayer for you as you read this book is this: that you get comfortable with not knowing the right thing to do. We don't know how to do everything, and we all make mistakes. A lot of times when I made a mistake, I would punish myself. But that is not a good way to live. Life isn't meant to be easy. If it were, we wouldn't need prayer, or spirituality, or healing at all.

I was meant to make my mistakes so that I could grow to be nourished, to learn and become a better person for my family and my community.

As these indigenous ways surrounded me more and more, I realized my purpose was to help people through these ways. It was teaching me to teach others. I learned that I don't carry these ways; these ways carry me. It comes without ego to walk the Red Road because there's no place for ego. It teaches you to see everything and everyone as a relative. Mitákuye Oyás'iŋ is the word for the oneness of everything that has been created by Wakȟáŋ Tȟáŋka, the Great Mystery. This is only the beginning, and from here we will journey together to learn and heal . . . no matter where you are from, whatever language we speak, we'll learn to see each other as relatives. It's up to all of us to make this life a good one.

INTENTION

The intention for this book is to grow communities. This book teaches the Native American philosophy as a way for people to find their way back to their own natural spirituality and healing. In fact, healing is just the process of finding our way back to our original design. It can help you come to terms with the embarrassing and wounded parts of yourself—and realize exactly who you are meant to be and your purpose on this earth. This book was born out of prophecy. Each message began as a prayer and was answered in ceremony.

Your indigenous spirituality can help you come to the realization that you don't have to go through a lifetime of suffering to find a sense of connection and peace. You can get there simply by listening to your innate spiritual guidance. We all have it, whether we call it our conscience, our intuition, our moral values, or our virtues—it is already downloaded within us when we are born. We can feel in our hearts whether something is right or wrong. This doesn't need to be taught. We all have this knowing; we just need to be reminded. We are all human, and we all come with this same understanding. This is natural law, this is spiritual intelligence, and that's what this book is about.

THE CREATOR'S LAW

We need to remember to balance natural law with the modern world and to reconcile our past with the present. These things are already perfectly balanced in us, just as the moon is perfectly balanced with the earth and the sun is perfectly balanced with the planets. And that balance—that self-actualization—has to start within us, with our own self-love and our own self-reliance.

If you're uncertain whether you're on the right path, whether you're reading the right book or making the right choices in life, the natural law of the Creator will guide you. Ask yourself, have you seen a dragonfly recently? The dragonfly is a messenger, delivering guidance from the spirit world to those who are on a journey of spiritual self-actualization. Pay attention. The moment you pick up this book and begin reading it, the dragonfly will begin to show up in various places in your life. And, like the dragonfly, our hope is that this book will show up in your life at the moment it is needed.

Our journey begins—as always—from within.

INTRODUCTION

INDIGENOUS SPIRITUALITY

To our elders, forgive me speaking before you;
I am young and still learning. Thank you for all
the things you taught us to keep these ways alive.

— Doug Good Feather

Many people are attracted to the humble ways and ancient wisdom of Native American spirituality; however, this book is not meant to teach people how to be "Native American." **The intention of this book is to help people build a bridge from their life in the modern world back to the deep ancestral roots of their innate spirituality.** In fact, if we were to journey back to our earthly ancestral origins, each of us would discover heritage and wisdom deeply rooted in the indigenous spiritual ways of ancient Europe, Africa, Asia, North and South America, the island nations, the Arctic nations, and other lands that now only exist in myths and legends. The goal of this book is to guide people on a personal spiritual journey to make this connection, using their own indigenous heritage, teachings, and way of life. Obviously, we may not all be Native American, but each and every one of us is indigenous to Mother Earth.

Indigenous spirituality is not a religion; it's a nature-based way of living in alignment with Mother Earth and the spiritual laws of the universe. The answer to any meaningful question can be found in the natural world if you learn how and where to look. Those who learn to *Think Indigenous* live unencumbered by any human's attempt to exploit and manipulate the intention of the Creator. Indigenous spirituality is both a practice and a way of life. No political party controls it, and no religious dogma dictates it; you can practice any religion and also identify with indigenous spirituality. As we learn to Think Indigenous, we're learning the principles of honor and compassion for all beings and how to integrate these principles into our daily life so that we can experience a powerful and beautiful relationship with the people and world around us. So let's begin where this journey started.

A VISION QUEST

This book came into being as a result of a prophecy that was shown to me while I was on a vision quest on Bear Butte, a spiritual place in the Black Hills of South Dakota that's been used for vision quests by indigenous people for thousands of years. In this vision, Great Spirit instructed me to share the ways of Native American spirituality to help people who are suffering and need to connect with the ancestral wisdom and healing of their own spiritual roots. Everything that this book is came out of this vision quest—which isn't to say that it's new. It is a synthesizing of so much history, along with so many stories, philosophies, and teachings from all over the world, gathered into one very profound moment.

That moment was not easy to reach, however. A year or so before my vision quest, I was suffering from debilitating PTSD, which one day brought me to be lying in a ditch on the side of the road, weeping. But someone came—a helping hand to pull me to my feet and brushed me off, lifting me out of the ditch. But when I turned around, no one was there.

A couple of weeks later, an elder came to me in a dream and told me to spend one year preparing for a vision quest—which wasn't something I had even considered attempting. The elder said to spend that year thinking about what I wanted to do in life—what impact I wanted to have on this world—and then to go to the Black Hills for answers.

On a vision quest, you put water away, you put food away, and you give yourself wholly to the spiritual way. You don't necessarily know if there will be life or death on the other side, but you put your trust in the Creator.

I fasted on the mountain for four days. By the second day, I was ready to give up. I felt that I was dying. And then, out of nowhere, I was surrounded by tiny butterflies, fluttering around me, holding me up. And my doubt and suffering disappeared.

The butterflies left and the suffering returned, but then another swarm came. Larger butterflies, in so many colors—blue, red, green—surrounding me with compassion and taking away my fear and pain. They guided me through that entire day, and what was actually hours felt like minutes. They gave me the strength I needed to stay on that mountain so I was able to keep the commitment I had made.

On the third day, a blue bird came at daybreak, singing a beautiful melody. As I listened, I was hypnotized by the blue bird's song, and it took me into my vision and the root and reason for my quest. The elder that had come to me in my dream appeared once more. The elder said, "It is good that you came. That was me that picked you up out of that ditch. We are going to show you your purpose—look."

The elder pointed off into the distance, and the ground I was standing on rose up. I could see all the people on earth, and they were in chaos and despair. "Look," the elder said. "You people make yourselves sick. In order for the people to heal, people must be willing to make sacrifices, and people must be willing to forgive and love."

THE BUTTERFLY PROPHECY

My vision is known as the Butterfly Prophecy, but similar prophecies have occurred in different cultures and been known by other names. These similar prophecies share three primary messages: First, that Grandmother Earth is in the process of bringing balance to human-caused ecological destruction. Second, that it is time for chosen keepers of traditional wisdom to build bridges between nations and share their indigenous wisdom to help heal and raise the vibration of humanity. Third, that there are many people from many nations and races who will recognize these ancient indigenous teachings and be a part of the healing and help humanity cross the threshold into this new era of deeper spiritual connection with Mother Earth and with each other.

The people referred to in part three of the Butterfly Prophecy are known as Star Seeds, people who have been planted here with an inherent sense of knowing of earthly and celestial spiritual flow. Star Seeds will feel the heartbeat of Mother Earth pounding in their chest as they read the strangely familiar words of the prophecy.

We are talking directly to you. This book is not in your hands by accident; you called these teachings to yourself.

THINK INDIGENOUS

Think Indigenous is the philosophy of traditional indigenous life, in service to the Great Mystery by helping to raise the vibration of love on Mother Earth. We're common men and nothing more. As Native American authors, we must state to our elders that we won't be speaking anything of the ways of indigenous secret societies, the highly guarded esoteric teachings, or our sacred ceremonies. We will be sharing only those things that we've been instructed to share—

indigenous stories, analogies, metaphors, lessons, and personal experiences as a means to help the reader reconnect with their own natural sense of indigenous spirituality. Indigenous spirituality is important in the modern world because this vast ancient knowledge can help us solve many modern problems. One of the reasons we have modern problems that we don't seem to have modern solutions for is as humanity has evolved, technologies have separated us from the natural world. We've drifted further and further away from the ability to recognize and connect with the source of our original spirituality. We no longer think in terms of immediate social responsibilities or long-term consequences to our unborn children—we think in terms of exploiting people and the planet with a degenerative cultural perspective and rapacious societal belief. The ability to Think Indigenous helps us reconnect with our ancestral spiritual knowledge, find a sense of balance in our daily lives, live in congruence with the environment, get clarity and understanding of our purpose, enhance our natural intuition and psychic abilities, and attract and allow all that is genuine and sacred. At this time in history, there may be nothing more important to humanity and Mother Earth than restoring essential elements of our indigenous ways of thinking back into our modern world and our daily lives.

Every indigenous culture has individual beliefs. What unites all indigenous cultures is the core philosophy of living in harmony with the ways of Mother Earth and in alignment with the natural laws of the universe. These core spiritual concepts are true for most human societies. Unfortunately, after the countless worldwide migrations of billions of people over many generations, a massive number of modern-day humans have lost connection with the spiritual origins of their ancestors. Though this connection has been lost to history, the spirit guides of these Star Seeds still hold vigil over the latent memory of the ways of Grandmother Earth and Grandfather Sky.

The fundamental nature of our collective indigenous spirituality is what unites us all as one people, and we can all rest assured that the Creator does not require anyone to be born Native American in order to understand how to Think Indigenous.

APPRECIATE, BUT DON'T APPROPRIATE

There's a fine line between the appreciation of a culture and the appropriation of that culture. To appropriate a culture means to emulate and imitate the distinct language, music, designs, symbols, rituals, traditions, mannerisms, and styles of dress that make up the defining elements of a specific group of people and their heritage. When someone who is not of a specific heritage steals any element of that culture, they are insulting and dishonoring the great love and loss, victories and defeats, and joys and suffering that were experienced and endured to achieve that distinct heritage and become that unique cultural identity.

Discussing Native American spirituality is a way to help people living in a modern world to connect with their own natural spirituality, but it is not an invitation for the reader to adopt Native American culture as their own. It is, for instance, deeply insulting and supremely ignorant for a sports team, school, company, or costume to appropriate Native American culture. Wearing a sports team's Native American logo or wearing a "Native" costume to a party or a war bonnet to a music festival is an act of outright racism. Again, it is good to appreciate Native American culture, but it is not acceptable to adopt or appropriate the heritage of it as your own, no matter the circumstances or intentions.

However, we can honor and use certain teachings, as they are universal to Natives and non-Natives alike. Terms like *the Red Road, in a good way, Sacred Hoop,* or *medicine* are shared by many cultures that span thousands of years, with only slight variations and meanings. These terms and words act as a kind of shorthand that we use to sum up something that has a lot of meaning without using a lot of words. It's okay for us to use these words and terms in reference to the context and teachings of this book. Let's get into some of these meanings now so we have a reference for the rest of our discussion on how to Think Indigenous.

THE RED ROAD

Many people come to a point in their life when they struggle with the purpose of their walk here on earth. They have reached a crossroads; it is here that they will discover the beginning of their *true* journey—walking the Red Road. Those of us who feel called to live life rooted in nature-based spirituality are said to "walk the Red Road." This simply means that we have certain universal truths and sacred principles that guide us as we live a spiritual life. The term also has meaning for people who use these universal truths and sacred principles to overcome great adversity in their life, like homelessness or extreme abuse or neglect, or for those who are courageously battling moral injury, anxiety, or depression or who face addiction but make a decision every day to live a life of sobriety.

In a Good Way

"In a good way" is a term that's used in conjunction with walking the Red Road. If "walking the Red Road" means that we are on a virtuous path of learning universal truths and sacred virtues, then "in a good way" means that our daily actions and behaviors are in alignment with those teachings, morals, and virtues. These ways are as profound as they are simple, they are as powerful as they are humble, and they are as sacred as they are common. These are living virtues that cannot be purchased, and they are not for sale; we either live them or we don't.

THE SEVEN SACRED DIRECTIONS AND THE THREEFOLD PATH

The Creator has laid down many paths to spirituality; *Think Indigenous* is just one of those paths. No matter which path we take, all of them end up teaching us about our spiritual connection as the creation of the Creator, why we're here and what we're meant to do.

The Sacred Hoop of Life and the Seven Sacred Directions that make up that Hoop of Life help us to understand life, and they expand our understanding of creation and the Creator. The Seven Sacred Directions—East, South, West, North, Above, Below, and Center—are powerful forces of universal energy that dynamically interact with everything that's in our environment and awareness as human beings. All these energies, spirits, forces—whatever names you know them by—are in constant movement with each other and with every being on Mother Earth.

In the final chapter of this book, we'll braid these strands of indigenous thinking into modern life through three related pathways composing the Threefold Path:

- **The Way of the Seven Generations:** *Conscious living* is a modern term for the ancient way of living in harmony with the laws of nature and how the personal choices and decisions we make will affect the lives of our unborn relatives seven generations from today. Conscious living also takes into account the many generations that have come before us, which stand as examples of what to do and what not to do so that we can avoid past mistakes and learn to allow joy and success to reach us faster.

- **The Way of the Buffalo:** *Mindful consumption* is a modern term for the ancient practice of respecting and honoring all beings on Mother Earth. We'll learn the practice of being intentional and deliberate with our impact on the earth and the beauty of walking on our journey of life with the awareness of a circular mindset. Mindful consumption is about our role in nurturing our self and being a steward of those things under our care.

- **The Way of the Community:** *Collective impact* describes the process of finding your truth and being a part of a like-minded community. We discuss how to elevate awareness and become a living example of truth in action. We also learn about activism and how to shine a light on the crimes being perpetrated against our Mother Earth and our relatives from every nation.

You will learn how to live a life that will help you to be happier as you build a powerful connection with these spiritual ways. There are many ways and paths to spirituality. This way is just one, but it is a good one.

CHAPTER ONE

THE CREATOR AND THE SACRED HOOP OF LIFE

The Creator has many names—God, Jehovah, Allah, Yahweh, the Great Spirit, and many more—yet they all converge on the universal concept of a divine energy. This energy is woven into the fabric of all we are and all that is, all that has ever existed or that will ever exist. The word we use in Lakota for this ultimate divine energy is *Wakȟáŋ Tȟáŋka*, or the Creator.

The Creator is neither male nor female, but the balance of all that is masculine and feminine. More specifically, the Creator has no fixed label or imagery but is the point of harmony and balance of *all* energy, including the point of singularity where all energy is expressed and accessible through a divine state of awareness. **The Creator is the awareness that allows both the existence of anything and everything and the contemplation of the existence of anything and everything. The Creator—the Great Spirit—is every-single-thing and the space between every-single-thing and the possibility and potential of every-single-thing.**

As the physical form of a spiritual being, each of us is a fully realized manifestation of the Creator that we chose to co-create. And our purpose in life is to express our self as the highest and best version of this life that we chose.

Since Native American spirituality is not a religion but a spiritual way of life, there is no "hell," and there are no rules, special conditions, or requirements to get a backstage pass into "heaven." In our physical, earthly life, the indigenous way of thinking is that we're on the Red Road, and when we've passed over to the camp on the other side— back in our fully spiritual form—we're on the Blue Road. Again, different indigenous cultures use various terms, but we honor our own ancestors by the name they use to refer to the collective consciousness of all beings: the Great Spirit. In modern terms, the Big Bang is simply a theory to help humans understand the moment the quantum (latent consciousness) became self-aware. The collective consciousness of all beings is known as the Great Spirit, and the *awareness* of that consciousness is known as the Great Mystery. The Great Spirit is the web of life, and the Great Mystery is where all things are created and where all things shall return. It's an indigenous version of heaven, but without the pearly gates or a saintly bouncer; it's simply "the other side" of this side. It's agreed that it's blissful and beautiful and perfect, but beyond that, it's simply a mystery to the mortal mind; our beautiful connection and relationship with the Great Mystery is learned through the lessons offered to us by Grandmother Earth and Grandfather Sky. When our time in physical form here on earth is complete, our body reenters the circle of life through the ways of Grandmother Earth, and our soul returns to the Great Mystery through the celestial realm of Grandfather Sky.

IS THE CREATOR REAL?

Whether we believe in the Creator or not is of little consequence, because the Creator exists at the very instant that we wonder if it exists. The very instant we conceive of something is the very instant that it's created. So, the moment we ask the question "Is the Creator real; does God exist?"—well, the Creator now exists.

Many people are not going to be satisfied with our insufficiently precise description of God, the Creator, or our rationale of God's existence. So let's get linear and logical.

The Creator cannot be broken down into a physics equation or a mathematical theorem. But for those who require evidence, that evidence may be discovered in the quantum. Classical physics deals with the properties and mechanics of the universe, that is, the physical things that are the result of particles and waves that exist in the physical realm. However, it's quantum physics that holds knowledge of the space that's in between those particles and waves, which is the unseen, the unknown, and the mystical.

When humans attempt to analyze the concepts and constructs of any ecological or natural system, a curious mathematical ratio appears again and again: the ratio of 1.618:1. This design ratio of $A/B = (A+B)/A = 1.618$ is seen everywhere in nature, whether in the form of a shell, the path of an electron, the horn of a buffalo, or the dividing and multiplying of cells. And it's not only found in natural systems; it's found throughout the anthropological history of our ancestors as well. The Egyptian, Aztec, Olmec, Mayan, and Incan peoples all used the ratio of 1.618:1 for the dimensions of their pyramids and other sacred structures. Modern-day academics don't know whether these ancient indigenous cultures arrived at their understanding of this hidden order through their relationship with and spiritual intelligence of the natural world around them or if they were taught by the Star People, or a psychic download from the lodge of the Sacred Beings, or by some other path. However, we do know that this design is found throughout the spiritual and physical realms since the start of recorded history.

This divine design found throughout nature—this ratio of 1.618:1—has been given many names throughout history: the golden ratio, phi, the golden mean, the Fibonacci sequence, and the Divine Proportion. And these are just some of the ones we know of. Indigenous elders tell us that some advanced mathematical knowledge and formulas predate their recorded existence by thousands of years, and still more exist but are not ready to be rediscovered for some time yet.

Underneath the nature of nature lives this mathematical design of 1.618, like a hint or a wink from the Creator. Inherent in its definition, a "design" implies there is a "Designer," or that someone or something created and encoded this design into the natural systems of the universe. The divine design of 1.618 is a fingerprint that's been left behind as evidence that the Creator is real. So whatever or whoever that "Designer" is to you, that is the Creator.

In our linear and logical world, many people need to see something in order to believe it, but for those walking a spiritual path, many times we need to believe in something in order to see it. Letting faith take the lead often comes with too much fear for many people, and they never experience that which they so need. The analytical and authoritarian minds of the world desperately seek to institute order and control over any sign of wild and divine chaos. As a result, without a strong sense of faith in our chosen path and belief in our journey, we may feel unprotected and vulnerable and left with a great desire to regain a personal sense of safety, control, and predictability in our lives.

Even if we intellectually know that any guarantee of safety, control, and predictability is an illusion in our modern world, our ability to ignore that—our cognitive dissonance—helps us to sleep at night and not totally freak out. The trouble is, without faith in our natural sense of spirituality—not someone else's version, but our own—the cognitive dissonance that gets us by in life will eventually manifest as depression and anxiety, leading to suffering and worse. Continually attempting to build walls and rules around spirituality and applying formulas and theories to it will keep us looking for a safe corner in a round room.

Spiritually disconnected humans attempt to structure the Creator into models and narratives, in ways that frequently benefit self-serving political and financial agendas. Industries and organizations—specifically politics, science, and religion—try to organize the Creator into systems and processes, rules and compliance, and rewards and punishments to make us believe that personal safety, control, and predictability lie within their particular brand of salvation.

But the world is already naturally organized in a sacred manner that has nothing to do with the opinions and assumptions of these people's industries, their governmental departments, or their religious organizations. The natural organization of the spiritual will appear as we ascend into our natural sense of indigenous spirituality. The divine proportion of 1.618:1 and other sacred geometries are the indigenous tongue of the quantum universe. And if we listen to the universe, it will guide us on a journey of spirituality where we may discover that we too have an original design and that we naturally fit into divine relationships and sacred roles that have already been set in place by the Creator.

Now we must focus on the pink righteous elephant in the room: religion.

Organized religion has had a death grip on our one-on-one spiritual relationship with Mother Earth for the last few thousand years. In essence, religions have hijacked our natural sense of spirituality. Religious leaders have led us to believe that they want us to have a personal relationship with God, but they create systems and processes that force us to go through their particular brand of corporate spiritual salvation.

It isn't that all religion is bad. In fact, anytime we gather and pray, we're acting in alignment with natural universal principles of connecting with Spirit through community and gratitude. And, of course, if an organized religion brings us a deep sense of peace, comfort, and connection with God, then there is no need to abandon that doctrine of belief in order to also Think Indigenous. But when we become comfortable enough to step away from religious dogma, we may experience that the Creator is still present even without the pageantry, punishment, rules, and doctrine of obedient belief that is so frequently a part of organized religion.

We are spiritual beings in physical form: we already know how to connect with Spirit; we just need to *remember* what we've always known by relearning how to think like our indigenous ancestors. And in order to begin to think like the ancestors, we must first begin to understand the sacred movement in which all life has a place and a part: the Sacred Hoop of Life.

THE SACRED HOOP OF LIFE

We know from science and from Spirit that everything is made of energy and that all energy is potential energy. We can't make more energy, and we can't delete energy, as it simply transmutes itself from form to form. It's also said that energy acts as light until it's observed, and then it's experienced as matter, which is another way of saying that we can change the energetic signature of that which we observe by changing our intention. Native people talk of the connection between spirituality and energy through the story of the Sacred Hoop of Life, because it's this story that teaches us about our spiritual relationship with the universe. Human life, as with all energy, is a continuous journey through doorway after doorway in a continual sacred spiraling movement. The relationship that self-aware beings have with the movement of this divine energy is known as the Sacred Hoop of Life.

The Sacred Hoop also represents the sacred movement of all things that are part of the quantum web of consciousness. That sounds complicated, but it's really simple. Think about it this way: **A hoop is created whenever any two things come together to form a relationship. It could be two people, two atoms, or two forces of nature—any time two or more entities share a space, a hoop is formed, and the sacred laws of the infinite circle bind the relationship of that hoop.**

All life is but a fractal of ever-expanding and multidimensional concentric circles within circles, collapsing and replicating in the never-ending story of birth and rebirth. At the center of the Sacred Hoop of Life is our distinct and unique self. Each of us is a point of singularity, the literal center of our universe, as an extension of the immortal Creator expressing itself as a mortal human creation in the form of you.

From the center, at our own personal singularity, flows each of the four cardinal directions, and we are also that point of connection where the earth joins the sky. Together, these powerful forces of universal energy make up the Seven Sacred Directions—East, South, West, North, Above, Below, and Center. Each of us is a sacred space through which every part of the universe flows to offer itself for reflection and to offer answers, perspective, and meaning to our lives.

As a sacred instrument of creation—like the hollow bone of an eagle—we hold this space where the above merges with the below and the sacred directions intersect and pass through one another. We are the space in that center; we are the eye of the storm. Holding space for this harmony of universal energies—this Sacred Hoop of Life—requires awareness, vigilance, and practice. It requires us to Think Indigenous.

> *Then I was standing on the highest mountain of them all, and round about beneath me was the whole hoop of the world. And while I stood there I saw more than I can tell and I understood more than I saw; for I was seeing in a sacred manner the shapes of all things in the spirit, and the shape of all shapes as they must live together like one being. And I saw that the sacred hoop of my people was one of many hoops that made one circle, wide as daylight and as starlight, and in the center grew one mighty flowering tree to shelter all the children of one mother and one father. And I saw that it was holy.*
>
> — HEȞÁKA SÁPA (BLACK ELK)

As we journey through life, we build our sacred hoops, and our hoops join other sacred hoops, and together these hoops form a sphere. The sphere is a divine shape that occupies space in three dimensions, yet its measurement—pi—is infinite. The sphere is the original form of the Creator, holding space for all other forms of creation.

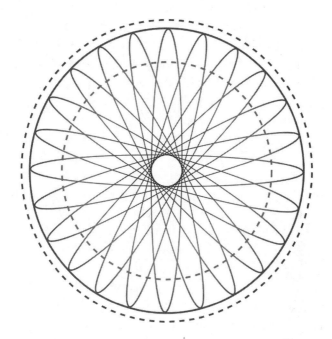

The Sacred Hoop connects us with that sphere, the All. There is nothing that we do in life that solely affects that particular thing we're doing. Every action we take creates a cascading series of reactions that continue far beyond our ability to perceive them and can have serious impacts that we cannot conceivably predict.

This common understanding of the Sacred Hoop of Life allows us to further expand upon and explore the ancient indigenous knowing of the sacred birth and rebirth of all energy in the universe.

MITÁKUYE OYÁS'IŊ

Mitákuye Oyás'iŋ is an indigenous Lakota phrase that has a combined meaning of "we are all related" and "all is connected." There are various ways to pronounce this phrase, depending on the circumstance, but the accepted informal version is pronounced "Me-talk-oo-yay Oy-yaw-sin." This phrase refers to that connection between hoops and spheres, that all beings and all things, both seen and unseen, are interconnected and intrinsically related. Not just humans but the totality of every single thing.

Mitákuye Oyás'iŋ—we are *all* related and we are *all* interconnected—*all* of us: the two-leggeds, the four-leggeds, the swimmers, the crawlers, the wingeds, the tree people and all those who grow roots, the stone and mineral people, the elementals . . . everyone. This also includes the forests, rivers, oceans, prairies, deserts, mountains, and valleys . . . everything. Mitákuye Oyás'iŋ is a prayer of harmony for all forms of medicine, spirit, and life.

Essentially, the best way to approach Mitákuye Oyás'iŋ is to simply be kind with each other. We can always adapt as events play out between each other, but our first point of engagement with each other should always be to be kind with each other, because we *are* each other and we all share the same mother: Mother Earth. She's our connection with each other and the embodiment of kindness. Kindness is the spiritual default of those who walk the Think Indigenous path.

MEDICINE

There's a lot of misunderstanding and misinformation about the word *medicine* as it's being taught and misused by plastic shamans, New Age gurus, and pretendians. And, to be clear, we certainly don't mean the pharmaceutical industry's misappropriated use of the word *medicine*.

Medicine is **essence**, and essence is the most distinct and concentrated characteristic of a singular thing. Each distinct thing in this world has a natural energy, and natural energy comes in positive and negative forms, as well as masculine and feminine forms. Essence is created when bonds are formed, and essence is released when bonds are broken. These bonds can be in the form of relationships, ideas, molecules, or any assortment of instances when things come together or come apart.

When two good things join together, the essence that is created is good medicine, and it is the foundation of love, health, and healing. Good medicine can be anything that promotes healing, well-being, and love and can be as simple as smiling at someone who may need it (even if it's smiling at our self in the mirror). Even our mistakes can be medicine, because if we learn from our mistakes, then we can teach others the lessons of our mistakes, and helping people is good medicine. Good medicine is spending time with a good friend or animal relative, walking in nature, swimming, making love, laughing, enjoying a good meal, or having good thoughts and wishes for someone. Molecules can be another example of good medicine. A hydrogen molecule by itself is distinct, and so is an oxygen molecule; however, when these molecules bond in a certain sequence, they create a medicine that allows all life to exist—H_2O, or water. Good medicine is the essence that's created when at least two things come together and create something good and positive.

When two bad things come together or are broken apart, the essence that's created or released is bad medicine, which is the source of anger, pain, and suffering. For example, bad medicine is created when two people with negative needs come together and create an abusive relationship, such as two highly co-dependent people forming a relationship that results in enabling and abuse. Bonds can be broken apart with bad intention and release bad medicine, such as when governments split the atom to use in weapons of mass murder or when parents break apart and use their children as leverage to inflict pain and suffering on each other.

Then there's the question of what happens when a good thing and a bad thing come together. When good and bad come together—as they often do—the essence is imbalanced and out of alignment. The reason a good thing and a bad thing are attracted to each other is that each is missing something the other half wants. Maybe one thing has a need to control, and the other has a want to be controlled. Or maybe one thing gives a certain type of safety or attention and the other thing needs a certain type of safety or attention. Someone who has been sexually abused in their past may find themselves in a relationship with someone who may not be good for them or make them happy, but who has the physical ability to protect and provide some sense of control and safety. When someone feels a void, they will seek to fill that void. When a positive and a negative energy come together, the bond is weak and unstable, but the inevitable breaking apart of that bond can be explosive. The way we heal that void is to work on reconnecting our spirit with the ancient knowing that each of us is already perfect, whole, and complete just the way we are.

Now that we have a base understanding of indigenous medicine, we can now talk about Spirit.

SPIRIT

Spirit is the collective embodiment of various medicines working together, creating a distinct spiritual entity or environment. Imagine a body of water made up of countless water molecules. This body of water can be in the form of an ocean, a river, a lake, or a puddle. **Spirit** is the result of all the medicine that body of water is supporting, nurturing, and holding space for. If we are talking about the spirit of a river, we're talking about the collective being that is the total combination of the medicine of the microbes teeming in the nutrient-rich riverbed, the medicine of the insects clinging to the underside of the river stones, the medicine of the water plants taking in carbon dioxide and giving off oxygen as their gift to other beings, and the medicine of all the beaver, fish, frog, and turtle people that the sacred water holds space for. The collective medicine of all those beings living in harmony with one another in that space is called Spirit. Similarly, the collective medicines that make up a forest is the spirit of that forest, the collective medicines that make up a tribe of people is the spirit of that tribe of people, the collective medicines that make up a mountain is the spirit of that mountain, and so on and so forth.

Spirit is the natural harmony and organization of Grandmother Earth, and when we disrupt this natural harmony, we create suffering and imbalance. When we need an abundant source of energy as a society, we take it from a limited resource of dead energy, such as oil or gas. Then we create suffering and imbalance that eventually spirals into various disasters and diseases. Building dams stops the migration routes of our salmon relatives, creating cascading instances of suffering and imbalance across multiple ecosystems. Creating suffering and imbalance is often the result of the ignorance and the handiwork of those infected with the disease of corruption and greed.

We can help to bring harmony and balance back to the spiritual ways of Grandmother Earth, starting with connecting with each of the Seven Sacred Directions of the Sacred Hoop.

THINK INDIGENOUS

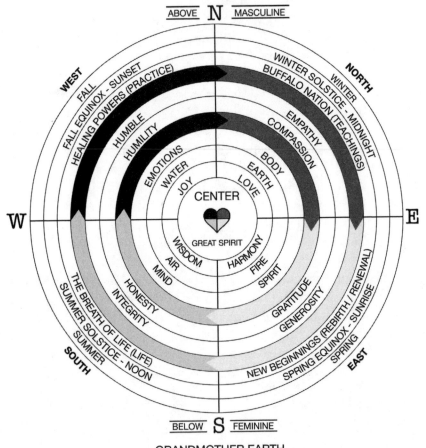

GRANDFATHER SKY

ABOVE **N** MASCULINE

WEST

NORTH

FALL
FALL EQUINOX - SUNSET
HEALING POWERS (PRACTICE)

WINTER SOLSTICE - MIDNIGHT
WINTER
BUFFALO NATION (TEACHINGS)

HUMBLE
HUMILITY

EMPATHY
COMPASSION

EMOTIONS
WATER
JOY

BODY
EARTH
LOVE

CENTER

W ———————————————————— **E**

WISDOM
AIR
MIND

HARMONY
FIRE
SPIRIT

GREAT SPIRIT

HONESTY
INTEGRITY

GRATITUDE
GENEROSITY

THE BREATH OF LIFE (LIFE)
SUMMER SOLSTICE - NOON
SUMMER

NEW BEGINNINGS (REBIRTH / RENEWAL)
SPRING EQUINOX - SUNRISE
SPRING

SOUTH

EAST

BELOW **S** FEMININE

GRANDMOTHER EARTH

CHAPTER TWO

WIYÓHIŊYAŊPATA —EAST

NEW BEGINNINGS

Behold, my brothers, the spring has come;
the earth has received the embraces of the sun
and we shall soon see the results of that love!
Every seed is awakened and so has all animal life.
It is through this mysterious power
that we too have our being
and we therefore yield to our neighbors,
even our animal neighbors,
the same right as ourselves, to inhabit this land.

— Tȟatȟáŋka Íyotake (Sitting Bull)

SPRING

As life circles the medicine wheel, signs begin to appear and the thunder beings awaken the land, alerting all beings to wake up and begin again. Our deer and elk relatives drop their antlers, and the bear elders leave distinct paw prints on the banks of the rivers and lakes as subtle signs that the sacred movement of all things is shifting into a new season. In the spring, the thunder and lightning people arrive with their unmistakable message to be vigilant as Grandmother Earth is renewing the ceremony of life.

For us humans, these months hold space for our regeneration, our rebalance, and our rebirth. Essentially, this time is fertile ground for new beginnings. This is more than a beautiful sentiment, for if we can learn to intuitively sense the changes in the natural renewing energies of this season and begin to live in alignment with the sacred movements of the earth and moon, the power of these seasonal and celestial events will breathe new life into us in profound and powerful ways.

We're in a time when many people the world over have spiritually devolved and have lost connection with their seasonal and celestial senses. The good news is that it's not difficult to rebuild our relationship with the ways of the earth and stars. The memory of these ways is literally part of our ancestral blood memory. When we learn how to sink into the rhythm of our natural spirituality, we can sense the influence the moon has on us, and we become keenly aware of our earthly relationship with the power of the sun. We may have forgotten the words of our original song, but we can hum along until we begin to remember again.

This time of rebirth and renewal comes with a sign from the most powerful and raw source of elemental energy: the sun. The sun is the bringer of light, and everything that is born from light begins in the East. The East is the sacred direction where we greet the sun and the light of a new day. Each and every morning offers us a chance to start anew, fresh, and to begin again. Each morning when we wake— should we choose to listen—is a message from the Creator to remember the privilege we were given of waking up. It's a reminder to get up and prepare our self, to honor our self, to go out into the world, to connect with Mother Earth and the hearts of other beings, to inspire and encourage those who cross our paths, and most importantly, to enjoy life.

The journey the sun makes across the sky every day is more than a common celestial event; it is a universal experience and powerful medicine that's shared by every being on earth. If humanity were to collectively honor our gift of a new beginning every morning, it would be enough to heal the world. The sun is one of our greatest medicines: it's our hope; it's our giver of life; it's a healer. Sadly, much of humanity may not appreciate the sun on a daily basis, but the quickest way to learn to appreciate something that we take for granted is to suddenly lose it.

When a solar eclipse is coming up on the calendar, it's a topic of conversation all week. There's the usual rush to find the cardboard glasses, and the people in their schools, workplaces, and homes go outside, gazing at Father Sky, watching the moon eat the sun. There are collective oohs and aahs as the sun disappears for a few minutes, as this brief event reminds us of our natural spirituality and rejoins us with our sense of awe and wonder.

But think about it—the sun only disappears for a few minutes! It leaves for hours and hours every night! Imagine what it would be like to have that same sense of awe and wonder when the sun returns every single morning of our lives. We need to connect with that awe, with that sense of gratitude and reverence *every day*.

Moments of celestial balance teach us about the earth's romance with the sun, where we can learn lessons of harmony, reciprocity, and balance. Solstices offer us the chance to contemplate the longest and shortest days of the year, helping us see that even the biggest activities in the solar system honor the natural law of reciprocity in that nothing is fixed on the spectrum of potential, but all life is in constant motion from the planetary forces. An equinox is when the length of the day and night are equal, like the nearly imperceptible pause between the inhale and exhale of the thousands of breaths we take every day. Humans take nearly 1,000 breaths per hour; the planets in our solar system just take longer breaths.

It's the spirit of the East, with its song of new beginnings and unrealized potential, that compels us to open the gate and let our spirit freely accept the past to move forward to new beginnings.

ELEMENT: PȞÉTA—FIRE

All of creation was designed to be in harmony with the Sacred Hoop of Life. The Creator made the rabbit people's ears like furry canoes for impeccable hearing and stretched their feet for great speed and precise maneuvering. The owl people were designed with feather regalia to fly more silently than any other bird relative and extraordinary eyes that can see through the dark robe of night.

Each being was born perfect for their environment and their role in life on this earth. But one day the Creator noticed that one nation had developed a terrible affliction. It was the two-legged people. The Creator discovered that Iktómi, the trickster spirit, had snuck into the earthly dimension and whispered into the ears of the sleeping humans over and over, "What's in it for me? What's in it for me?

What's in it for me?" When the humans woke up the next morning, the question of "What's in it for me?" was burned into their hearts and minds, and they now possessed an ego, which infected them with the delusion of entitlement and superiority. Their egos made them capable of unimaginable destruction and also afflicted them with an irrational fear of things they could not see or understand. Before having an ego, they were at one with and an intricate part of nature, but now they not only felt separate from nature, but they felt separate from each other. The Creator felt pity for what had happened and took mercy on the two-leggeds and gave them four elemental gifts powerful enough to help bring balance to the tragedy and burden of their egos: fire, water, air, and earth.

The element of the East is fire. From the moment we received our gift of fire, its warmth and light became the center of our lives. We've prayed and shared meals around a fire, we've shared tales and taught lessons, we've celebrated our victories and lamented our defeats, we've told our stories of birth and rebirth, and we've created meaning and memories with each other. Around a fire is where we remember those who have come before us and we wonder about those who are yet to come. Fire represents the fundamental principles and building blocks of humanity: warmth, safety, security, food, family, and community.

Fire is a powerful philosopher. If a human needs their ego put in its place quickly, then just give them fire and let them treat it with dishonor and disrespect. Fire brings balance to the human ego because it can quickly deliver an unforgettable lesson on the vulnerability of our human condition. The element of fire forces the human ego into submission, as it has no regard for our ego's need to feel in control of our surroundings or superior to other beings or nature in any way. When we work with fire, we're really working with honor and respect, the universal paradox of creation and destruction, and the spiritual themes of birth and rebirth.

The very nature of fire is its perpetual cycle of transmutation, purification, and renewal. This is why it's the element that represents the East. The behavior of fire that destroys in order to create reminds us how precious and impermanent all life is. This helps us to remember that we're all in this together and that we belong to something bigger than ourselves, that we belong to each other. Ultimately, we're all just walking each other back home to the Great Mystery.

INDIGENOUS VIRTUES: GRATITUDE AND GENEROSITY

Gratitude and generosity are similar virtues, but they differ in that gratitude is an internal characteristic and generosity is our external expression of our sense of gratitude. **Basically, gratitude is how we feel, and generosity is how we express that feeling out in the world.** Indigenous spiritual teachings associate gratitude and generosity with the East because of that sense of destruction and rebirth; if we find ourselves in a situation where we've given in to the hole of despair, the best way to stop falling is to pull the rip cord and deploy our internal sense of gratitude, then turn the negativity into positivity by immediately engaging the world in an act of generosity. To renew, to refresh, and to begin again is the lesson the East offers us. Let's go a bit deeper into each of these virtues.

Gratitude

When we engage with the world from a place of gratitude, it's the difference between trying to make something happen and allowing something to happen. The defining difference between effort and effortlessness is the virtue of gratitude. We see the quotes and memes from the sages and gurus that talk about gratitude. But why is gratitude such a core concept of joy, contentment, and well-being in our life? The ancestors tell us there are two primary reasons. The first is that a person cannot exist in a place of fear and true gratitude at the same time. The second is that gratitude is the doorway to divine intuition, which allows us to be guided by our connection with the Creator.

Gratitude moves stagnant energy when we're feeling stuck in life. The simple act of practicing gratitude disrupts negative thoughts and changes our mindset to see the world in a positive way. Not only are we more attractive to others when we live in gratitude, but the most ordinary things can become extraordinary, creating a fuller, more beautiful expression of our life.

You've probably heard the old saying, "Things don't happen to us, they happen for us." Gratitude is the foundation of that adage. It means that our mindset has to be that the universe is generally conspiring and working in our favor. Frequently, when something that we perceive as "bad" happens to us, we let it affect us in a highly negative way. But if we interact with the world from a place of gratitude, when something happens that others may perceive as "bad," we just see that experience as "interesting." We are curious about why something happens the way it does, and in expressing that curiosity, we're actively seeking the part of the experience that we're grateful for. That experience was our destiny, part of the choice we made when we came into this life. Once we recognize the lesson, the natural laws of the universe will stop these types of experiences from happening.

Generosity

In Native American culture, generosity is a way of life, built on the communal value of equality. But in cultures built on colonialism, equality is not a value; instead, value is found in ownership, in the exploitation of resources for profit, in hoarding wealth, and in leveraging power over others. This has meant that in many parts of the world, generosity is seen not as a value but as a sacrifice. In the colonial mindset, when we're generous and we give something to someone, we see it as losing something, or perhaps as an exchange, as if our gift were something we can now hold over that person. Instead, in indigenous cultures, we see our generosity as honoring that person, or helping to heal and ease their suffering, where our gift will increase their dignity, happiness, or joy.

Our ancestors tell us that when we are generous with what we have, our own opportunities will expand in proportion to our genuine desire to help others. The medicine we seek for ourselves can be recognized in our offerings to others.

SPIRITUAL PRACTICE: INTENTIONAL PRAYER

What is prayer? Many people feel a disconnect from the practice of prayer, so let's start with a visualization.

Imagine the soul as a beehive. The hive is a pristine design of creation. It is home to a cloud of black-and-yellow fuzz balls suspended in various moments of arrival and departure. These bumblebees flying in and out of the hive are prayers. Some bumblebees are leaving the hive with our desire for protection, clarity, healing, and favor for others and ourselves, and other bumblebees are coming into the hive carrying the prayers that other people and our ancestors have sent to us.

Prayer is how we express the vision we hold for the highest and best good for any being or experience. We can pray for our self, for people we know, for someone we see in passing, for any animal, for a forest or a body of water, or for any situation going on in the world. We can pray to bless the path and the journey so that it will end in the highest and best outcome for that being or experience. Our prayer may be in silent reflection, in spoken words or song, or in a type of ceremony. And we can literally pray for anything.

Praying has nothing to do with being religious but has everything to do with being a spirit in human form. We don't need to be religious to pray, or for our prayer to be heard. Prayer is the language of the spirit world and is not attached to time or distance. It's possible for a prayer on one side of the world to be at work on the other side of the world the moment that prayer is offered.

THE STORY OF THE UNCLE SPIRIT AND THE NEPHEW SPIRIT

A young nephew spirit and an elder uncle spirit are sitting on a star, watching the earth. The elder is teaching his young nephew how to tune in to the frequency of the two-legged people. All of a sudden, the young spirit jumps up, holding his hands over his heart, yelling, "Uncle! I can feel them! I can feel them!" "Very good," says the elder spirit. "Now hold that vibration and allow your eyes to loosely gaze on their planet." The young spirit starts hopping up and down and pointing at the earth. "I can see something! I can see something!" The elder spirit asks, "Tell me, young one, what do you see?" The youngster describes millions of orbs of light coming out of the atmosphere and floating into the universe. "Uncle, those orbs are all quite beautiful, but what are they?" The elder replies, "Those are people's prayers." The young spirit watches for a bit longer, then asks, "Uncle, why are some orbs small and dim and others are big and bright?" The elder replies, "That's people's faith."

HÁU, MITÁKUYE OYÁS'IŊ

The times when we wish the most for guidance—"I don't have clarity around this issue"; "I don't know what to do"; "I don't know where the money is going to come from"— these are the times when we pray, when we hand the whole thing over to the Creator. That surrender of prayer allows us to realize that we're a part of a natural system, and under that system, everything is going to be okay. Remember, the universe is *for* you. It allows you to realize that you can handle all that you are carrying. The path of self-actualization—or a direct relationship with the Creator— can be found through prayer.

There are many ways of conversing with the Creator, as it simply means communing and conversing with our self. Consider using **intentional prayer** to connect with the Creator— this is a simple and direct way to connect with the source of our spirituality. But in order to do this, we have to deeply connect with ourselves. When we feel called to the process of "finding ourselves," it simply means that we feel pulled to connect with our authentic self and genuine nature. It's not meant to be some mysterious or esoteric activity. "Finding yourself" is simply finding clarity among many different perspectives of who we really are—and the best thing you can do for someone else is to work on becoming the best version of you. Because when you work on becoming the best expression of yourself, you don't have to chase things you want the most; instead, those things will chase you.

Start by connecting with your authentic voice. To do this, simply close your eyes and lips, relax quietly into the mind, and be with yourself, calming and quieting the watery landscape of your thoughts for a minute or two. Once the water is calm, simply and intentionally say, "Hello." Then do it again, and sit with the thought: "Who just said that?" It's your voice from another dimension. That is the voice we use to pray intentionally and personally connect with the Creator.

THE SPIRITUAL PRACTICE FOR INTENTIONAL PRAYER

When we pray with intention, we don't focus on *how* our prayer will be answered, but instead we stay focused on the *what* and *why* of our prayer, because if we're caught up on *how* or *when* our prayer will be answered, then we're really just getting caught up in the make-believe scenarios of how and when our human desire wants something to happen and not on how the Great Spirit needs it to happen to be in alignment with the Sacred Hoop of Life. The Creator is not in a hurry; we are. We need to have faith and allow the divine laws of the universe to deliver us what we need based on our highest and best good.

In the first couple of lines of the Spiritual Practice for an Intentional Prayer, we're calling in our Grandfather and Grandmother, which are respectively the collective wisdom of the cosmos and the healing compassion of the earth. We'll use this outline to connect our genuine voice with our intentional prayer and repeat it over and over. When it begins to flow effortlessly, we can customize it and make it uniquely our own. Here's a basic outline for an intentional prayer that focuses our energy on asking for guidance with a troubling issue.

1. Begin by calling in your council of spirit guides.

   Grandfather, I'm calling on you; I need your guidance now.
   Grandmother, I'm calling on you; I need your guidance now.
   Ancestors, I'm calling on you; I need your guidance now.
   Creator, I'm calling on you; I need your guidance now.

2. State your prayer in simple terms.

   I am facing [INSERT TROUBLING ISSUE], and I don't know what to do. I bring this issue to you for your guidance. Please bless this prayer with clarity, protection, and favor for the highest and best good for all.

3. Pray for Mother Earth.

   And please bless our Mother Earth with healing and protection and ease the suffering of all her children.

4. Close with gratitude and remembrance.

   I am grateful—Mitákuye Oyás'iŋ

CHAPTER THREE

ITÓKAGATA–SOUTH

THE BREATH OF LIFE

Listen to the air. You can hear it, feel it, smell it, taste it.
Wóniya Wakȟáŋ—the holy air—which renews
all by its breath.
Wóniya, Wóniya Wakȟáŋ—spirit, life, breath,
renewal—it means all that.
Wóniya—we sit together, don't touch,
but something is there;
we feel it between us, as a presence.
A good way to start thinking about nature . . . talk to it,
talk to the rivers, to the lakes, to the winds
as to our relatives.

— Tȟáȟča Huštè (John Fire Lame Deer)

Summer

A whisper on the breath of Mother Earth sweeps across the world with a message to all her children that now is the time to celebrate life. Those who are spiritually tapped into the Sacred Hoop of Life can sense the essence of this breath. It is fresh and pure, filled with the wonder and exploration of baby foxes jumping and playing in a field of wildflowers. In many ways and in many places, the celebration of this breath of life is honored through ceremony.

In Lakota, the word for the sweat lodge ceremony is "Inípi," and it means "to live again." The sweat lodge itself is a small domed structure, made of willow branches and hides or blankets, where an ancient Lakota spiritual purification ceremony is held. This ceremony honors all life and is an act of spiritual renewal. There is one physical doorway to enter and exit the lodge, but the ceremony consists of four spiritual doorways that are aligned with the four directions of East, South, West, and North.

The South doorway is where our ancestors, elemental spirits, and other spirit guides enter from the spirit world. South, and its corresponding spirit world, is represented by the color white. White is the light that's in all of us and is a reminder that we must first learn to see light in our self before we can truly see the light in others.

In lodge, we pray in various ways—sometimes in silence, sometimes in spoken word, and other times in song. Indigenous people have always known the power of voice and the importance of the words we choose to use. One of the greatest lessons the ancestors have given us is this: **what we speak, we create.** Our words are powerful, and they can heal as well as destroy, which is why we must be mindful of the intention behind our words and use our voice for good.

One voice can encourage many voices to rise up, and many voices can merge into one voice and change the world. We witness the power of our collective voice when we go to concerts; we feel the power of the band onstage while the sea of people in the audience are all riding the same emotional vibration, singing together and feeling the growing energy field of the words and music. We go to concerts to come together as a community and to celebrate life with others who are part of the movement the music has created. There are even times when the concert isn't so much a performance as a spiritual ceremony, as the power of the event can wash away the stress and anxiety we feel, revealing genuine joy, reminding us of what's really important and who we're meant to be.

Our souls are drawn to celebrations because our indigenous spirit yearns to celebrate life. Modern society has created an unhealthy work-life balance, and it's so unnecessary. If we're being honest with ourselves, most of the jobs that we do don't contribute to the essence of life or Mother Earth in any significant way. They matter in the sense that they put food on the table, and, of course, there are significant roles that make up the backbone of our communities— mothers, caretakers, healers, teachers, and artists, and those who provide food and security. But too often we get caught up in our jobs and don't realize that much of the time, we're doing stuff for the sake of doing stuff. We're so busy going, going, going and doing, doing, doing that we forget to simply breathe and *be*.

Millions of people are waiting too long to celebrate life. They are spending their lives detached from Spirit and suffering from a sense of quiet dissatisfaction that's always lingering in the background. It's imperative that we stop making the mistake of thinking we have more time than we actually do, because one day it will be too late. We're alive at this very moment. Celebrate that fact, however you want, in any way large or small. In that celebration, slow down and notice the beauty of life itself. Do something thoughtful, do something exhilarating—just let the universe know that you're still here, that you're alive and *kicking*.

ELEMENT: ONÍYA—AIR

Air is the breath of life. It is the second medicine, the second gift from the Creator. We receive this gift, our first blessing from the world, the moment after we're born, when we inhale our first breath. The first prayer we send out into the world is our first exhale.

From that day forward, every day of our life, whether we're awake or asleep, every breath we take is a blessing, and every breath we release is a prayer. Each breath of life is an opportunity to reconcile and reconnect with our spiritual journey. The gift of air should never be taken for granted. Unlike fire, air cannot be controlled, captured, or contained. Without air, we cannot make fire. Without wind, the water in the oceans cannot transmute into the rains to water the earth. We can live without many things that sustain life for days, or even weeks, but we cannot live without air for even a couple of minutes.

Wind is air in motion. It can come in many forms, from a whisper to a mild breeze to a howling, hurricane-force gale. Wind is the powerful, unseen force that animates the world around us, teaching us lessons in gentleness, strength, awareness, and perseverance. Sending our breath on the wind through a flute creates a melody that can make us cry or make us dance. A gentle breeze rocking a new sapling tree back and forth ever so slightly and consistently strengthens the root system so that it is able to withstand the storms that it will face throughout its life. Later in life, the wind will take the leaves off that tree as fall turns into winter. The wind will bring the rains as spring turns into summer. Wind is the unseen hand of constant change, sent to us from the spirit realm.

Both the wind and the South represent the invisible forces of our heart, mind, and spirit. Indigenous elders say that wind can signify that a change is coming; a big wind can be a sign of a big change. But we can affect this change ourselves by turning air into wind, wind into breath, breath into words, and using those words to speak our desires into reality. All too often, we forget that the element of air and the power of the wind have valuable lessons and wisdom to offer us. And all it takes is simply to sit still and follow our breath or listen to what the wind has to tell us.

THE STORY OF THE FUR TRAPPER

Five hundred years ago was a time of great change for the indigenous people of Turtle Island. The Eastern territories had been invaded by foreign European hostiles, and the Europeans were sweeping West, claiming and colonizing anything and everything their eyes fell upon. The indigenous people of the lands to the far North had very little interaction with the colonizers at this point, and so they didn't yet realize the destruction that these strange new people from across the great waters were capable of.

One day, a pale foreigner dressed head to toe in animal pelts entered the indigenous people's camp with a translator from one of the Southern nations. The translator arranged an audience with the council of elders, and the foreigner explained that he was a world-renowned fur trapper and had traveled several moons to meet these elders. He had heard the tales and legends of the great bounty of resources of their land and wanted to establish a trade route to extract the resources of the land and take them to the markets in the East. The fur trapper told the elders that he would make each of them very rich.

The elders did not understand the desire for a human to sell the blessings and beings of Mother Earth to make a few people rich. The council tried to teach the fur trapper that the land and the animal relatives of the land belonged to no human. They explained that their council acted as the guardians of the land, and, as such, they denied his request and asked him to leave.

The trapper had already considered the elders could deny his request, but he also knew that he could count on their well-known generosity and hospitality, characteristics the colonizers exploited often. The elders granted his request to trap some beaver so he could have pelts to trade for food and supplies on his journey back home. The fur trapper was led to a valley deep in the mountains with three very specific instructions: "Trap in this valley and nowhere else, only take what you need for your journey and nothing more, and leave by the next full moon." The trapper agreed and gave his word.

The fur trapper quickly learned that the legends and tales did not even come close to the treasure trove of animals available for the taking. Not only was there every highly desired fur pelt imaginable in the valley, but the beavers alone numbered in the hundreds. He began trapping immediately and trapped from early in the morning until late at night. He couldn't empty his traps fast enough before they were full once again. The trapper couldn't even sleep at night, because the beavers slapping the water with their tails never stopped, but he would find sleep every once in a while with a big smile on his face, knowing the riches that were piling up due to all the fur pelts. The trapper swept through the valley with his iron traps as the time he was told to leave drew near.

A few days before the upcoming full moon, the council of elders asked about the pale-skinned man they had left in the valley. The scouts reported that the trapper had not yet left the valley, nor was he anywhere close to the only practical entry and exit point. The elders sent a band of warriors to track down the fur trapper and escort him out of their homeland. The first thing the warriors discovered was that the trapper had killed nearly every single beaver in their sacred valley. He had bundled up their pelts and hidden them in the caves that were scattered throughout the valley, because there were simply too many to haul out in one trip. The warriors quickly found the trapper's trail and picked up speed, knowing the fur trapper was a few days' ride ahead of them and they needed to close this distance fast.

At this time, the trapper was becoming anxious knowing the elders would send warriors to find him soon. But his guarantee of being powerful and wealthy beyond measure was only a couple hundred more beaver pelts away. How could he stop when he was so close to such a huge fortune? As he lay awake in bed listening to the slapping of the beaver tails on the water and calculating how many more beaver pelts would be required to achieve this fortune, a single howl pierced the night. The hair on the back of his neck stood straight up, and he scrambled out of his tent.

It was a wolf relative, and the howl was so long that it seemed impossible that this was a single animal. Then, another howl and another howl joined in from various parts of the valley . . . he realized that he was surrounded by wolves. He broke camp and left immediately. The trapper would travel for a time, and then he would see a couple of members of the wolf pack, which would force him in another direction. A bit later, he would see another few members of the pack off in the distance, and that would force him in yet another direction. This went on throughout the day and night and drove him to exhaustion.

At twilight on his last day, all sounds in the forest went silent. The fur trapper heard a faint rustling all around him, and glowing eyes appeared. There was no time to run. He jumped off his horse and scrambled to the top of a cottonwood tree. The trapper made it to safety, but the faithful horse under his care did not, and the wolves took up position all around the cottonwood. The trapper had faced off against many different predators before, and he was resolved that these wolves would not be having him for a meal anytime soon. He reassured himself that he was a famous trapper known for taming the wild and savage lands of this new frontier and reminded himself that women idolized him, children called him a hero, and lesser men wished they were like him. The wolves would make runs at the tree and attempt to claw their way up, but they were simply not built to do this.

The trapper began taunting the wolves that they were no match for his greatness and should just give up and go away. And, after a couple of days, some of them did. The remaining wolves stayed and stalked the tree, never allowing the trapper to come down or run away.

On the fourth day, the warriors had caught up and positioned themselves on a ridgeline a short distance from the wolf pack and fur trapper, watching. It was the night of the full moon, and it was so bright it looked like silvery daylight shining on the forest. All of a sudden, the wolves began to howl, and as each wolf joined, their crescendo grew, and fear turned the fur trapper's blood into icy river water. The circle of howling wolves parted as the alpha returned with their relative, the beaver. They made their way to the cottonwood tree, where the beaver slowly ambled to the base of the tree that held the fur trapper. The wolves circled the tree as the beaver got to work. Just before the tree started to fall, the trapper gave up hope and began crying. The warriors came and chased off the wolf pack and returned the trapper to the camp and took all his fur pelts. They gave him food and allowed him to rest. The council then met with him telling him of his wrongdoings and banished him from their lands. He returned home with a lesson and his life.

HÁU, MITÁKUYE OYÁS'IŊ

INDIGENOUS VIRTUES: WÓOWOTȞAŊLA NA OWÓTȞAŊLA—HONESTY AND INTEGRITY

Honesty and integrity may seem like terms that are interchangeable, but they're really quite different. Honesty is an internal moral value, while integrity represents the actions we do in our everyday lives. The Lakota associate honesty and integrity with the South because the spirit realm has the highest level of interaction in our life when we're most free of self-delusion and self-righteousness. This clarity comes from our self-work of clearing the obstacles that obscure our sense of honesty and integrity.

This work entails seeing and celebrating life and understanding who we are meant to be. It means working with the lessons of the second medicine, and it takes getting our mindset positioned in a good way. Observing our intentions from a place of honesty and acting with integrity in our day-to-day life are the lessons the South offers to teach us. Let's look further into each of these values.

Wóowotȟaŋla—Honesty

At some point, we may have promised somebody something that made us sound good and righteous, but we honestly knew all along that we weren't going to do anything we said we were going to do. Sometimes, desecrating our honesty is done consciously, but sometimes we sabotage ourselves unconsciously. This can show up in scenarios as significant as putting people at risk, betraying someone's love or trust, or it may show up in small situations like telling little white lies. Either way, being dishonest is unnecessarily destructive in many different ways, and even the smallest piece of dishonesty will impede us on our spiritual journey. Besides, being honest simply saves everyone a lot of time. But we must explore our sense of honesty—or the honesty of another person—very carefully, because complete honesty comes with a powerful clarity that we may not be prepared to handle.

Honesty is an internal value, and it requires a tremendous amount of work to clear away all the lies, excuses, and stories we tell our self to keep us protected from seeing ourselves as inadequate, unimportant, or vulnerable and to avoid accountability to our self and others. It isn't easy, but if we don't do the work to come to terms with our internal sense of honesty, we will continue suppressing our ability to see our self with total clarity. Most of us love the *concept* of complete honesty, right until it's time to be completely honest with our self. But this level of complete honesty is the most significant step we can take on our journey to self-actualization—the point where we are living up to our potential through the universal principles of harmony, wisdom, joy, and love.

Being honest with yourself can oftentimes be painful, but the more you avoid it, the longer your problems will persist and the more they will grow out of control. The best way to begin is the simple practice of admitting when you've made a mistake; the first person you have to admit your mistake to is yourself. It may seem easy to admit being wrong, but it's not. Throughout our lives, we've taught ourselves to build armor around all the broken and embarrassing little parts of ourselves that make us weak and vulnerable to the systems of the modern world and the people in it. We need to overcome those tendencies, and Thinking Indigenous and walking the Red Road in a good way will help us to think and act from a genuine place of honesty in our lives.

Owótȟaŋla—Integrity

Having integrity simply means clearly communicating what we're going to do and then doing what we say. If we consistently act with integrity, it will build admiration, and people will trust us. If we act without integrity—if we break our promises or go against our word—then people won't respect or trust us. It's that simple. When you crumple up a perfect piece of paper, no matter how hard you try to smooth out the wrinkles, it will never be perfectly smooth again. Integrity works in much the same way.

In the times of our ancestors, integrity was imperative because if you said you were going to help do something, or build something, or bring something, or be somewhere, your integrity could literally be the difference between life and death. Your word was your bond and essential to the health and well-being of indigenous society. The stakes may not be as high in the modern world, but our integrity is still the primary value that defines our character and how we've chosen to show up in the world. We don't have a say in whether or not we have integrity, and it's not something that we can just declare; having integrity is something that only other people can say about us.

There's no gray area when it comes to having or not having integrity. It can take a lifetime to build and the blink of an eye to lose. When it comes to integrity, the old ones say that we should live our life in such a way that if someone spoke badly about us, no one would believe them.

SPIRITUAL PRACTICE: TȞAWÁČHIŊ—MIND

The South sends us a message on the wind to celebrate life, for doing so will help keep us on our journey of Thinking Indigenous and leading a spiritual life. But we also have to acknowledge that "celebrating life" can be an idealistic concept for a lot of people. There are times, in all of our lives, when everything feels like it's falling apart, and it can be hard to find something we want to celebrate. Many people live in a constant state of anxiety and struggle, and they live that way because society feeds their minds a constant diet of thoughts composed of fear and scarcity. Their worst enemy is the constant internal dialogue going on right between their own two ears; they feel they never have enough of anything (self-esteem, self-confidence, good health, opportunities, money, etc.), and they live in the fear of countless imaginary what-if scenarios.

Those thoughts then manifest as recurring themes throughout their lives. They spend their time on this earth lamenting their past, desperately justifying their present condition, and fearing their future. They never seem to fully engage in any significant level of meaningful or lasting joy, contentment, or success. They drift between bouts of apathy, waves of anxiety, and the on-again, off-again search for some kind of meaning. It may be that living in these conditions is neither good nor bad, that these are the lessons they are here to learn in this life. But, as we discussed earlier, if you *learn* those lessons, you get to move on from being presented with the same ones over and over again.

If we are able to step away from fear, we can be abundantly content with what we have—whatever it may be—and find the ability to celebrate life. Those who have found the way to do this are operating at the level of a dedicated Spiritual Warrior. Mind you, they don't spend every day sliding down rainbows and frolicking with unicorns, but for the most part they're enjoying a higher-than-average quality of life. Spiritual Warriors tend to be intrepid explorers, pioneers, trailblazers, teachers, thought leaders, and creators. They seek a charged life—a life of passion, purpose, and divine work—and they often have a message that's beating inside of them that they need to get out to the world.

Why are they this way? It's because of *how* they think. They have distinct passions that they cultivate, bringing them to advanced levels of spirituality. These Spiritual Warriors are driven to serve humankind with their talents, gifts, and messages to the world. We've all met these people, and we can all see that they are simply *different* . . . but *why* are they different?

The answer is because of the way they see the world, and how they see themselves *in* the world. It's their mindset—which is a way of being conscious of the way we create our own reality. Without a developed mindset, we *unconsciously* create our reality, and then when we struggle and suffer in our lives, we can't figure out why. Remember that no matter the circumstance, we are always just one decision away from a totally different life; we just need to *make* that decision. That decision can be as simple as adopting a brand-new mindset, one that will radically shift our perspectives.

Here are some basic things that we can stop doing that will immediately impact our life in positive ways:

- Stop judging others and yourself.
- Stop criticizing others and yourself.

- Stop comparing yourself to anyone else.

- Stop being responsible for other people's problems.

- Stop living your life trying to please other people.

- Stop being dishonest with yourself and others.

- STOP living life like you'll do it "someday," because you don't have as long as you think you do.

Procrastination can be our worst enemy. We tell ourselves that we're going to do something that we know we need to do, but we don't, and we knew all along that we weren't actually going to make the time to do it.

Essentially, procrastination is having a lack of integrity with our self. There are always other factors at play, like exhaustion at the end of the day and the emotional damage we put ourselves through with anger and thoughts of inadequacy, but those all feed into procrastination. You have to make that decision . . . and then *do* it. A powerful solution to overcoming procrastination is an ancient practice that comes from the South, the element of air and the second gift of the Creator: our breath.

Our breath is the birthplace of intention, and our intention is the foundation of our mindset. Great battles have been won and lost in the mind before a single warrior ever walked onto the battlefield. Success or failure is decided in the mind before a business venture ever gets launched. Enduring love and abject heartbreak are determined in our mind before fidelity ever builds its nest in our heart space. When the topic of spirituality and breath work is discussed, the first thing that usually comes to mind is meditation. A traditional meditation practice takes a dissociative and observational view of our thoughts and actions, but that's not the state of being we need to summon when we celebrate life. Our intention is not to disconnect from these things; rather, we want to vibrantly connect with our mind, body, and spirit in order to summon energy at will. We want to heighten our senses to allow ourselves to engage the world with the highest and best version of who we are and what we're becoming. The Breath of Life Method is the counter-balance to traditional meditation in that it's meant not to disassociate and observe but to activate and engage and light up our physiology at will.

THE BREATH OF LIFE METHOD—HOW TO QUICKLY ENERGIZE YOURSELF

This practice will highly oxygenate your blood very quickly. Your eyes will need to be closed, so it's important that you're in a sitting position and able to hold on to something to steady yourself. When you're done with the practice, don't stand up right away. You may get dizzy and fall down. This practice can energize your whole physiology in less than a minute and its effect may last for an hour or more, so it's important that we don't practice this method too close to when we need to go to sleep.

1. Close your eyes and allow your forehead, eyebrows, jaw, and shoulders to fully relax.

2. Through your nose, fill your lungs with a slow and deep breath.

3. When your lungs are full, hold your breath, and then *open your mouth*. Quickly inhale with a short powerful breath, and fill your lungs to their maximum capacity. This is called "filling the bellows."

4. Hold that breath for seven seconds, and then exhale quickly and forcefully.

5. Repeat steps 1 through 4 four times, and then open your eyes ever so slightly and take a slow and deep breath—not focusing on anything in particular—just a soft, downward gaze as you feel your senses heighten, your energy rise, and your body come alive.

When you're done, stand up slowly. Every breath you take is a gift from the Creator. Let's offer a silent thank-you and give gratitude for the gift of the second medicine: our breath.

CHAPTER FOUR

WIYÓȞPEYATA– WEST

THE HEALING POWERS

*When a vision comes from the thunder beings of the
west, it comes with terror like a thunderstorm; but when
the storm of vision has passed, the world is greener and
happier; for wherever the truth of vision comes upon
the world, it is like a rain. The world, you see,
is happier after the terror of the storm.*

— Heȟáka Sápa (Black Elk)

Fall

Just as the sun begins to set at the end of the day, so does the
season begin to set on the cycle of the medicine wheel. As
summer retreats into our memories, the South wind brings
the fall and offers us this time to reflect on the intentions
we had for the year and what we've accomplished thus far.

It's a time to finish our projects, to reap what we've sown, and to prepare all that we've harvested as we move into the next season of life.

Fall is also the time to gather our family and community together, to share in our blessings, to help others, to tell stories and visit our memories of the past year and remember those who have crossed over before us to the camp on the other side.

The West is where the Thunder Beings—the Wakíŋyaŋ—come from. They fill the atmosphere with rolling thunder, brighten the senses with lightning, and bring the healing medicine of the cleansing rains. The Thunder Beings come from the spirit world; they are the Creator's warriors, and they come to teach us vigilance and to heal sickness in the world. The Thunder Beings are allies to the Star Seeds, those sacred humans that have picked up the ways of natural spirituality. Carrying these ways can be a heavy burden at times, and the Thunder Beings help to give us healing and strength to hold that space for Spirit to come through us as we continue to walk the Red Road in a good way. But, just like when we walk any road, we gather dirt and grime along the way, and we need to wipe it off. The Thunder Beings' medicine can wipe us off spiritually and turn water into medicine. A shower, bath, or swim can wash away the stress and worry and cleanse those things that are sacred. They help keep us clean from drugs and alcohol and other forms of self-abuse.

Humans have the tendency to look the world over in search of spirituality and self-healing, but time and again, no matter how much we look outside ourselves, it's the power of the sacred teachings and the power of the West that help us understand that what we're seeking is not to be found outside of our self, but that all divine understanding has been within us all along.

ELEMENT: MNÍ—WATER

Water is the first medicine. We were conceived through water, we grew and were protected in a womb of water and we were birthed into this world through a sacred water bearer. Water is the first medicine and earth (or rock) is the first creation. In a Lakota sweat lodge, the sound we hear when the water is poured on the rocks is the sound of the universe. This is not a poetic metaphor; this sound is literally the sound of the universe. When scientists recorded deep space for the first time, that sound—the sound of the first creation connecting with the first medicine—is the sound that they heard. Indigenous peoples have known this is the sound of the universe for thousands of years.

Many modern scientific tests have resulted in the discovery that water expresses sentient qualities, meaning that water responds to positive and negative energy. Water forms beautiful or distorted crystals, and plants thrive or fail to thrive, depending on the positive or negative energy it's exposed to. As humans, we're composed mostly of water, so if speaking kind words and sending positive energy to water can change the molecular structure of water, imagine what speaking kind words and sending positive energy to our fellow humans can do. Or, for that matter, any sentient being. We barely have any understanding of the true spiritual power and wisdom of water. Water is a teacher, a healer, and the source of all life. All water leads directly into you. There is nothing more important than water to the health and wellness of every sentient being on Mother Earth.

The West is associated with emotions as well as water, because both are fluid in nature. We cry salty tears from our emotions. Emotions are tied to our sixth sense, and working with our emotions is part of the work that humans need to do to open up our psychic senses and join all the other sentient beings on the planet that may not walk upright but are tuned in to the psychic world around us.

WAKÍŊYAŊ NA ÍYA—THE THUNDER BEINGS AND THE GIANTS

On the Standing Rock Indian Reservation, there's a lowland area out on the distant plains called *Where the Thunders Hunt*. It is a land of deep ravines and rocky outcroppings and a maze of deep underground caves. The valley received its name from a harrowing event that happened between the Lakȟóta Oyáte (the Lakota people) and the Íya Oyáte (the giant people) in the distant past of pre-America. Both nations lived on the plains, but they did not live in harmony. The giants, an ever-present danger to the Lakota people, were about twice the height of a human and would come into the villages at night to steal women, livestock, and children.

One day, a hunting party of the Lakota's finest warriors were out on an extended hunting trip when a messenger from the village rode up in full gallop. The giants had come into the village and taken several people and animals. The warriors immediately mounted up, and led by their best tracker, they found the giants' trail leading far out into the vast prairie.

After two days of tracking, the warriors found the entrance to their cave just as the sun was passing the highest point in the sky. The warriors had been told many fireside stories of the giants and one of the things they had learned was that giants slept during the day and woke from their slumber shortly after sunset, which meant that they didn't have long. The stench of the cave was overwhelming. Just inside the entrance of the cave was a giant that was supposed to be on guard, but who had fallen asleep. With the possibility of the sleeping giant waking up at any moment, the warriors worked quickly and quietly to free those who had been stolen from the village—at least those who were left.

The warriors and the freed relatives rode hard and fast to put as much distance as possible between themselves and the giants. When the giants eventually woke up and discovered their meals had been taken, they exploded into a violent rage. Howling and roaring, the clan of giants poured out of their cave, hungry to catch whoever stole their food, rip them to shreds, and feast on their bones.

Giants have keen senses, and once they picked up the scent of the warrior's horses, the chase was on. They quickly closed the distance. In the moonless night, the warriors could hear the howls and roars of the giants coming for them. The horses were exhausted and the village was still over a day's ride away. The warriors knew there was no possible way they could make it home before the giants overtook them.

Desperate and faced with mortal danger, they could have given up, but they didn't. One thought grounded them and put their overwhelming fear in check: they remembered that they were the sons and daughters of the ancestors who gave everything so they could have this beautiful life and continue to live these beautiful ways. The bone-weary group dismounted and gathered in a sacred circle next to the creek they had been following. They took out their čhaŋnúŋpa wakȟáŋ, their sacred pipe, joined the bowl with the stem, and gathered in prayer. They prayed as the giants drew closer, and they could hear the giants' bloodcurdling cries in their strange, guttural language. It appeared that all hope was lost for this small, noble band of Lakota.

The people took a buffalo horn filled with water from the creek, and they blessed themselves by drinking the water and wiping themselves down. The medicine man held the sacred pipe up to the sky and prayed: "Thunder Beings of the West, we're calling on you. We need your help now. Please protect us, guide us, and watch over us. The people of the giant nation will be upon us soon and will kill us. Protect us from these giants, and defeat them for us through your power. We want to live and see our family and our loved ones and walk this beautiful Red Road in a good way. Creator, this is our prayer. Mitákuye Oyás'iŋ." They smoked the sacred pipe, honoring all seven directions.

And the Thunder Beings came.

Clouds began to form in the distance, billowing and growing until they stretched across the horizon and quickly began to black out the star-filled canopy of night. Thunder rumbled across the prairie and shook the ground like a hundred thousand stampeding buffalo. The whooping and howling of the giants went silent and when the lightning flashed, the Lakota could see that the giants had stopped their charge and were huddled together in fright, frozen and not sure what to do.

A huge group of thunderclouds rolled out over the prairie sky and settled directly over the clan of giants. Lightning flashed inside the massive thunderheads, and with each flash, they could see the huge outline of a figure in the clouds and knew this was Wakíŋyaŋ Wičháša— Thunder Man. He had brought the Thunder Beings to help the people. Thunder vibrated everyone's bodies to the core and lightning filled their eyes with every possible color of light. Thunder Man spoke to the medicine man, telling him to get everyone on the horse relatives and go home with eyes forward and not to turn around for any reason. They did as they were told.

Thunder Man called upon the Thunder Beings to cast bolts of lightning all around the giants as they turned and lumbered as fast as they could back to their valley. When the giants got back to their caves, they were so frightened of the power of the Lakota's prayers that they sealed up all of their caves and went deep into the earth and back to the underworld.

HÁU, MITÁKUYE OYÁS'IŊ

The indigenous teachings of the West are powerful, because lessons of this sacred direction are rooted in the most elemental parts of what makes us human. The West represents the full spectrum of our raw human emotions. It represents our first medicine of water, it's the sacred direction that holds the space for our joy, and it's the direction that holds two of our greatest morals and virtues as a human— humility and humbleness—both held together by sincerity. Sincerity is the keystone trait that provides the strength in our relationship with the spirit world. Our prayer is often the strongest when we're experiencing our greatest fear, because that's when we're praying with pure sincerity. In the story of the giants, it wasn't the level of danger that allowed the Lakota to summon the powerful Thunder Beings. It was the sincerity of their prayer.

INDIGENOUS VIRTUES: WÓUŊŠIIČ'IYE NA IGLÚHUKHUČIYELA— HUMILITY AND HUMBLENESS

Ninety-nine percent of all life on Mother Earth is smaller than a bumblebee. And if we remove anything from the natural order of our Mother Earth, no matter its size, something else will suffer. But there is one exception. The one thing we can remove to improve the world is humans. The ecological environments on this planet do not rely on humans in any way to survive and thrive. Our Mother Earth only suffers supporting our human life, and she would be better off without us humans on the planet. Therefore, we need to be deeply grateful that we are so provided for and approach our relationship with our Mother with humility and humbleness for her love and generosity.

We can learn about humility and humbleness the easy way or the hard way, but we will learn this lesson one way or another. If our minds are breeding grounds for corruption and our hearts are filled with greed and we justify our taking and taking and more taking, then Mother Earth will come and humble us. It would be easier on us if someone a bit gentler, like an elder, a wisdom keeper, or a medicine person, could offer us this lesson. When Spirit is the one to humble us, it can bring us to our knees before it picks us back up—that is, if Spirit even decides to give us another chance at all. The council of elders told the fur trapper to only take what he personally needed to make the journey back to his land, but he ignored these instructions. Instead he made the journey back home with a lesson in humbleness and humility.

Wóuŋšiič'iye—Humility

There's a thin line between confidence and arrogance—it's called humility. It's been said that humility is not thinking less of our self but simply thinking of our self less. The ancestors tell us that the way to develop our inner humility is to practice being outwardly humble. A lot of people think it's dangerous to be humble, because in the modern world, if we're not outstanding in some way, then there's always someone faster, brighter, and more than eager to take our job or steal our intimate relationships away from us. Most of us can't afford to be without a job, so we manufacture ways to make our employer think that we're somehow indispensable. The same could be said for our behavior in our intimate relationships and in our social circles, with qualities that we pretend to embody or perceived shortcomings that we hide from the world.

There will come a time when the Creator will call us home. This is a fate that we'll all ultimately experience. It doesn't matter where we live, what we drive, how much money we have, or how many followers we have on social media. What does matter is that we examine why we feel these things are important and why we feel the need to impress people. These two questions will help us get to the heart of our issues by contemplating our humility.

Humility is one of the most difficult qualities to sense in people, because by its very nature, it is concealed. But we can get a sense of humility when we run across a genuine leader. For example, the modern-day typical "leader" makes us feel like *they* are important when we meet them. But when we meet a great leader, they make us feel like *we* are important. Great leaders don't try to impress or convince anyone of how important they are. They're just common people who are engaging life from an inner sense of humility and that humility shines through in how they show up in the world.

Humility is essentially getting out of our head and not allowing our thinking to always begin with "What's in it for me?" It allows us to elevate our senses above the white noise of society and see beyond just what's in front of our face. Humility opens our hearts and minds so that we are able to receive wisdom and information from the universe rather than just accepting the pseudo-wisdom and contrived information that scrolls past us on a daily basis. Humility is powerful enough to disarm an ego that's out of harmony with nature.

There are many ways to develop humility, but it starts by thinking about other people. We all think about other people all the time, but we think about them from our own standpoint, our own emotions. Instead, we need to learn how to feel and seek to understand what other people experience in their lives. This helps us learn and explore our own feelings about patriarchy, institutional racism, or corporatism—all of which greatly harm the sentient beings on this planet in one form or another. Humility is what allows us to do something or say something and genuinely mean it because we deeply understand and care for that thing. Humility is the cornerstone of integrity, sincerity, and humbleness.

Iglúhukhučiyela—Humbleness

Humbleness is closely linked with humility, as one cannot be humble without humility. The difference is that humility is an internal state, while humbleness represents the actions we take in the world. No amount of acting will make us humble; we can only genuinely *be* humble. That's why humility is important; without humility, being humble is only something we're pretending to be, and the only person we're actually fooling is our self. Engaging in life from a center of humble intentions is a behavior that will help not only us but also pretty much everything and everyone on the planet that comes in contact with us.

Learning humbleness is a practice that's ingrained in the indigenous way of life. This is embodied by the Lakota sweat lodge, where the top of the entrance is little more than a couple of feet above the ground. This is intentional, so that we may humble ourselves by crawling into the womb of Mother Earth on our hands and knees. We enter and exit the sacred sweat lodge in much the same manner as that in which we entered into this life—not walking upright like an adult and with our adult outlook of thinking we know everything, but crawling like an infant, truly vulnerable and spiritually open to the lessons of the universe.

SPIRITUAL PRACTICE: ČHAŊTÉ—EMOTIONS

Star Seeds, or Sacred People, are bright lights in an otherwise dreary modern society and they draw others to them like moths to a flame. People pick up their energy, holding on to it for years or even decades. The trouble is that the reverse is sometimes also true. A Star Seed often retains the energy from those they interact with, for better or worse. So someone with trauma can pass the emotional memory of that trauma on to us without being aware of it.

And, of course, we all have our own traumas. This is a natural part of life, as life isn't meant to be perfect and is instead meant to be useful. But if we allow that trauma to mean more than it does, it will always haunt our minds, whispering all the little story lines of our victimhood to remind us that we don't deserve happiness, that life has little meaning, or that we're not as good as other people. It's extremely harmful to constantly be in a loop of our negative self-talk, negative self-esteem, negative self-confidence, and all the social anxieties that go along with them. We must remember that every cell in our body is listening and reacting to how we talk with our self.

Most trauma comes from "unresolved emotions." This is an oversimplification, but it does give us a starting point to talk about issues rooted in a horrific event or conflict from our past that are continuing to affect us in the present. Often, during the traumatic experience, these negative emotions are imprinted on us psychically, as well as through our senses—our sight, hearing, smell, taste, and touch. People who have been sexually attacked often cringe at the thought of being touched on their necks or stomachs or arms or legs, and they frequently live without a sense of personal safety, unable to set or enforce personal boundaries. Many combat veterans can become paranoid and may have a tendency to create chaos when things seem to be "going really good" or get too calm and predictable.

These behaviors may be subconscious attempts to revisit the traumatic experience in order to heal it or reconcile it with some type of meaning, but we are rarely able to do so and instead the cycle of abuse continues. The elders tell us that the best way to get over something is to go through it. Part of that process requires coming to a personal sense of closure with the emotional energy of the trauma, including our emotions around the person who may have caused the trauma. This allows you a release from letting the trauma control you.

THE WATER TRANSFER

There are various rituals and practices that we can use to get closure. For instance, "burying the hatchet" is a phrase that comes from a time when certain Northeastern tribes would ceremonially bury their weapons and store them away to signify a close to their time at war and declare that they were now in a time of peace and healing. You may also be familiar with various "cutting the emotional cord" techniques that offer similar ways to help bring closure to our traumatic experiences.

The Water Transfer is a healing technique that works with our spiritual and energetic attributes—as we are spiritual beings composed of energy. In this practice, we cleanse and prepare our self, then conjure up the trauma and person or experience associated with the trauma. We acknowledge it and then transfer it to the water, allowing Mother Earth to take that trauma from us and put it away so we can move through it and get on with our lives.

Don't worry or question yourself with "Am I doing it right?" The important part is that you're meeting your prayer halfway by putting your intention into action.

This practice is not for everybody. If recalling your trauma brings you to a state of panic, put this practice on hold. And even though the Water Transfer has brought closure to and helped heal countless people, nobody is claiming that a lifelong trauma is easy to heal with a four-step healing practice. But even if it just helps get us through the month, or the day, or even the next five minutes, then it has served its purpose. It is highly recommended that this ceremony not be performed alone. This ceremony is best practiced with a trusted knowledgeable person.

1. **The Cleansing:** Pour 2 to 4 cups (1 to 2 pints) of water into a bowl. If possible, use a wooden bowl, but any bowl will do. Sitting on the ground or floor, pray with the water for a short time, connect with the water, tell it what you intend to do, and ask it for help. If possible, burn a little sage to cleanse yourself, the bowl of water, and the area. Then place yourself in a state of gratitude and take a drink of water from the bowl. Be very aware of every drop of the water coming into your mouth and down your throat. Using your hands, take a small amount of water and wipe yourself down to bless and cleanse yourself. Start at the top of your head. Lightly wipe your forehead, eyebrows, eyes, nose, and mouth, and move down over your throat and around the back of your head. Then lightly wipe down your torso, arms, legs, and feet.

2. **The Transfer:** Ready yourself by setting your intention for healing. Open yourself to be willing to let go of the trauma. Hold the bowl in your hands, and allow the experience of the trauma to come in. If a trauma comes in that you weren't expecting, don't try to stop it, because it's what is supposed to come forward. This step is about focusing on the trauma, even if it's difficult. This process is not for our human wants but for our spiritual needs, so don't second-guess any of this; just go with it. Keep your eyes open, and don't look away from the water during this entire time. Visualize every element of the trauma that came in—every sight, sound, and detail possible. Next, bring your awareness to your body and feel where in your body the emotions of this trauma

are coming from the most. Do you feel it in your stomach or your heart space? Are your legs tensed up, or is your throat dry, where you have no voice? Where is the energy getting stuck? Once you are aware of the area, ask the water to help bring healing into that part of your body. Sit with this part of the process for as long as you need, but don't take your eyes off the water. You'll know when it's time to move on. When you're ready, using every sense and with full imagination, you must grab hold of that experience from where it's stuck in your body and, with sheer will and intention, transfer it into the bowl of water. Take your time with this, because that trauma will be determined not to leave the home it has made in you. You will instinctively know when the experience is over and when the trauma is no longer a part of you and has become bound to the water in the bowl.

3. **The Closure:** After the transfer happens, close the visualization, and make sure to disconnect all senses. You're still looking at the water, but you're no longer imagining any images in the water, though the trauma is still bound in that water. Then take the water outside and pour it into the ground. If you have sage, it's good to burn a little to cleanse yourself and clear the environment. And you're done!

HÁU, MITÁKUYE OYÁS'IŊ

CHAPTER FIVE

WAZÍYATA–NORTH

EARTH MEDICINE

*The old people came literally to love the soil and they
sat or reclined on the ground
with a feeling of being close to a mothering power. . . .
Their tipis were built upon the earth
and their altars were made of the earth. . . .
The soil was soothing, strengthening, cleansing,
and healing.
That is why the old Indian still sits upon the earth
instead of propping himself up and away from its
life-giving forces.
For him, to sit or lie upon the ground is to be able
to think more deeply and to feel more keenly;
he can see more clearly into the mysteries of life
and come closer in kinship to other lives about him.*

— MATĦÓ NÁŽIŊ (CHIEF LUTHER STANDING BEAR)

WINTER

These are the months when we enter the time of the dreaming bear. It doesn't matter if you don't live in a place where bears do or if you live in a place where it doesn't snow—it only matters that you begin to become aware of the energy signature associated with this season. This is the time when the earth sends signals to her children that it's time to slow down, to define things that are unclear, to get organized, and to plan for the upcoming spring. Winter is a time of renewal, regeneration, and gathering with the community to share our knowledge, skills, and stories. It's a time to reflect on our lives and the world around us, to write down our plans, to create our vision boards, to ask ourselves what we need in the upcoming year, and to plant our intentions. This is a time to sit down with our significant others, our parents, and our children and ask them what we can do for them in the coming moons. This is the season in which we decide and rededicate ourselves to being disciplined in walking the Red Road, working with our medicine and with our people.

It's important to contemplate our understanding of and relationship with the concepts of nourishment and rejuvenation. We should also reevaluate the reasons why we're always hurrying and, especially, the meaning of intention. All of this is done with the knowing that spring is coming and, like the bear, we're preparing to emerge from our dens hungry, thirsty, and ready to engage the world once again.

The lessons of the North have to do with all the ups, downs, and everything in between of being a human being. The teachings of this sacred direction are connected with all the raw and primal elements of having a human body, having human feelings, and working through the daily human experience of this journey through the wild divine. Essentially, these lessons are the foundation of our human condition and the human endeavor.

ELEMENT: UŊČÍ MAKȞÁ—EARTH

The element of earth is another gift of the Creator and a foundational element of spirituality that offers us teachings on how to embody our human form. Meaning, earth is about practicality; it's about who we are, what we do, why we do it, and how we do it.

We can experience profound knowledge, miraculous healing, and deep contentment when we're able to connect with the wisdom and healing powers of the earth medicine from the North. There are ailments and issues in our lives that can only be learned or healed by having our bare feet on the ground, our hands in the soil, or our bodies in the water in quiet observation and with all our senses receiving the natural earth energy swirling around us. But people rarely, if ever, make the effort to connect with the earth in such a way. In our modern society, the most common way people connect with the earth is through some sort of recreational activity on a field of manicured grass or exercise on a well-worn trail, which is something, but it's not at all the same as or a substitute for a deep spiritual connection with the spaces we may find off the beaten path.

When was the last time you lay on the ground and gazed up at the sky while listening to the heartbeat of Mother Earth? So many people don't realize that we can actually hear the breath and the heartbeat of our Mother Earth. Some have never done this before and for others it may have been much too long since they've last made this connection. In order to understand nature, we have to dive in heart-first and that requires as much attention and earnest work as any other meaningful relationship in our lives.

In our world, there are people who not only have a deep spiritual relationship with earth energies but are able to communicate with them and use that ability to help others connect with profound knowledge and healing. Genuine healers say that they are not the ones healing anything or anybody; they are merely holding space for the people to connect with the knowledge to heal themselves. In fact, I say, "I am only an instrument through which Spirit connects. I'm a human man. If a person is not ready or willing to connect within, then they won't be able to understand this knowledge or be healed by this medicine. I have no authority to say who is, or is not, ready or able. That is for each person's spiritual council to be asked and accept."

When we're ready to connect with this type of healing and spiritual knowledge, we must be willing to work on our personal relationship with Mother Earth and Father Sky and our ability to Think Indigenous in a modern world. We'll discuss building a relationship with Father Sky a bit later, but our first question at this moment is, "How do we begin a spiritual connection with our Mother Earth when we're so disconnected from her?" Just as with any significant relationship, we have to work on our relationship with Mother Earth with great integrity, intention, reverence, and consistency. In other words, we have to fall in love with her.

She is the sand, rocks, soil, and all other similar matter that holds a nurturing space for practically everything on this planet. Imagine the sheer enormity of what it would feel like to be the home for all the sentient beings that live in or on you, as well as the cosmic level of love it takes to nurture every form of life.

Imagine the sight of the sunrise. There are stories of angels gathering at the dawn because of its heavenly beauty. And if you ever watch the sunrise, you'll see, when the particles of light hit each living cell of every being, how each light wave wakes up and brightens everything it touches.

But step away from the cosmic for a moment. The everyday things we do in life—cooking and eating, working and reading to our children, playing sports and laughing with friends—are as much a part of connecting with Spirit as the moments we spend in prayer. Our prayer is how we walk in this world and our life is our ceremony. This doesn't mean that every moment in our life is going to feel like it's being lived in perfect harmony. We can't hear that harmony up close—you'd have to pull back to the cosmic view again for that.

In order to remain a part of that silent harmony, we need to connect with our sense of dignity. Dignity is the earthiest of all human values and is associated with the North. Dignity teaches us how to embody our body while we're here in our human experience and doing the work of connecting to and building an intimate relationship with Mother Earth. That respect for Mother Earth starts with the respect we have for ourselves.

Our whale relatives were designed with no significant method of defense and are placed by the Creator to live in—by human standards—the most hostile environment on earth, the open ocean. The whale people show all other animal nations that genuine nobility does not require jeweled crowns, a manufactured aristocratic title, or even being an apex predator. The whale people elicit awe for being the living embodiment of noble dignity. People all over the world ride out onto the ocean to experience this dignity up close and personal. Genuine noble dignity is only possible with the total release of control. In other words, we walk away from our own sense of dignity when we allow or apply oppression on anything or anyone else.

We know what it means to respect someone for who they are, or for what they've achieved, or for the way that they do something that we regard as meaningful. Dignity is our inner sense of respecting who we are, what we've achieved, and how we behave. Essentially, dignity is how we respect our self.

Dignity is more than just our inner feeling of self-respect or self-confidence. It has both of these qualities, but it also includes an internal sense that we are worthy of the divine right of the very best that the universe has to offer in terms of love, harmony, wisdom, and joy. Dignity is the root-level value of who we all are as human beings. But many people find it difficult to feel this supreme level of self-worth because it requires a supreme level of self-love. The thing is, it doesn't matter what we've done in our past or where we're at in our life, because we are all worthy of a fundamental sense of human dignity. We are all a reflection of each other and our environment and when we negate dignity, we negate not only ourselves but the root value of all life on Mother Earth.

Human Dignity + Compassion + Kindness = Peace

If we remove human dignity, compassion, or kindness from society, there will be crime, conflict, and suffering, and there will be those who construct and claim some righteous privilege to own the land, to draw lines on maps and build walls based on race, ethnicity, and delusion. When society no longer honors human dignity, the diseased ones are able to easily convince us that the only solutions to simple problems are separation and war. And what is war but a source of revenue for politicians and a profit center for corporations? This is what is meant when we say the defilement or lack of dignity is the root cause of much of our human suffering.

Let's put our hearts and minds together and see what life we can make for our children.

— Tȟatȟáŋka Yaŋká (Chief Sitting Bull)

INDIGENOUS VIRTUES:
ÚŊŠILA NA WÓČHAŊTOGNAKE—
COMPASSION AND EMPATHY

Compassion is the ability to feel the same feelings another person is having. Empathy is when we take action to change another person's experience *because* we feel compassion for that person. We synthesize both compassion and empathy when we're able to step into the experience of another person, aiming to understand their feelings and perspectives, and then use that understanding to guide our actions. We embody compassion when we deeply connect with the understanding that another being is a reflection of us, and we embody empathy when we assist that being in practical, earthly ways.

Lilla Watson, an indigenous Aboriginal Australian elder, offers us these wise words of empathy:

> If you have come here to help me, you are wasting your time. But if you have come because your liberation is bound up with mine, then let us work together.

This is a powerful description of empathy, but what does it mean for our liberation to be bound up with that of another person? Martin Luther King, Jr., explains it further. While confined in a jail in Birmingham, Alabama, he wrote:

> Injustice anywhere is a threat to justice everywhere. We are caught in an inescapable network of mutuality, tied in a single garment of destiny. Whatever affects one directly, affects all indirectly.

The "inescapable network of mutuality" King is referring to is the potential humans have for compassion. Lilla

Watson's clarion call to action, "then let us work together," is empathy. Compassion and empathy allow us to come together as one mind, love with one heart, and move together in a sacred direction as one unified family. This is the power of the teachings and earth medicine of the North.

This is not to say that it's easy. What about all the bad people? What does it look like to work together to "liberate" those who intentionally and continuously commit harm? Are we going to convince the entire employee org chart of certain companies that just by doing their jobs, they are destroying the environment, promoting war, or harming the health and well-being of families? Of course not. Their paychecks are dependent on them *not* accepting that responsibility. How do we liberate these people? The answer is, we don't. We concentrate on those who are awakening and breaking free from these systems. These are the people we can help here and now. The ripple will spread from there and our collective vibe will eventually crumble the walls of these institutions and their way of thinking. This is the power of compassion and empathy.

Úŋšila—Compassion

We can directly experience compassion when we can look beyond the needs and circumstances of our own life and actually feel the feelings of another. Keep in mind that it's not always about feeling the pain and sorrow of another, for we can also choose to feel the happiness and joy of another. Compassion offers us the chance to practice focusing on all that's good and wonderful in the world. In order to help bring much-needed balance and symmetry to the world, make it a point to practice compassion with those who are suffering as much as with those who are experiencing joy and abundance.

While the ability to imagine what another sentient being is going through is important for bringing health and healing to our self and others, it is also one of the key human abilities that awakens and strengthens the psychic senses we used to share with nature and the animal nations. Through compassion, we create a psychic pairing with another being that's bridged through a space that no scientific instrument can detect or measure. And, as with any other type of practice, the longer we stay in that space, the better we become at working with the various energies of the psychic realm. Our compassion allows us to enter that space and develop our forgotten psychic senses.

Wóčhaŋtognake—Empathy

To internally understand what another is feeling will serve humanity well, but *when we want to do something about how we're feeling*, that action is called empathy. The most direct path to empathy is to realize that the other person or being *is* us. Empathy is when we take action to change another person's experience *because* we feel compassion for that other person. Empathy allows us to take action despite another being's species, race, nationality, or social class. When humanity engages our collective sense of empathy, we can move mountains.

It's true that empathy can motivate and mobilize the masses, but we can't just blindly take action every time we feel bad for something or someone. There are a lot of people perpetrating abuse and corruption in the world and an unlimited amount of wrongs to right, and we'd simply get burned out trying to step in and help fix them all. The old ones tell us that the key to effective empathy is responsibility and boundaries. When we get a sense of what's not feeling good, we have to realistically evaluate if we're in a position—and willing—to take responsibility for it. People who are highly empathetic often get burned by ungrateful people and burned out by helping too much. The key is to determine the best use of our energy and then set a limit on it. It's a big world with a lot of pain and suffering, so let's do what we can in a responsible way so we can do as much good as possible.

SPIRITUAL PRACTICE: TȞAŊČHÁŊ—BODY

Our body is a physical manifestation of creation in vibrant motion. In order to keep that vibration high, we need to be immersed in other naturally high-vibration elements of creation. If we live our life indoors or stay in the city for too long, we can get depressed. When we step away from nature, our mind becomes closed, our psychic senses dull, and our heart grows cold.

The spiritual practice for our body is to get back to nature to spiritually rejuvenate, reenergize, and heal. We have to relearn how to see with our "forest eyes." The key to contemplating nature is to see beyond the *form* of the beings in nature, which helps us to understand the energies that are required to have a system that exists in harmony. It helps us to understand the space and the beings differently. It takes a little while to sit with this concept and understand it, because we've been taught in the modern world that nature is just a pretty place full of resources for humans to exploit. Try looking at it this way: the deer did not cross the road, the road crossed the forest. See the subtle yet profound difference? That's the difference between seeing nature with a disconnected mindset and seeing Mother Earth through our forest eyes.

Máni Pȟežúta—Medicine Walk

A Medicine Walk is an indigenous practice that helps to create a spiritual communion between a human being and Mother Earth. The natural world is in constant communication all around us—we need to make the conscious choice to learn how to listen. Our ancestors would take Medicine Walks to seek signs, omens, and signals because the Creator speaks to us through nature. Even today, Mother Earth continues to offer us her insight, answers, and healing, and we can receive them through a Medicine Walk.

All that's required of this practice is to put our body in direct contact with nature, with no agenda and nothing to accomplish except to be fully present and intentionally connect with the vitality of the experience of the natural environment around us. Although this practice may seem obvious and something many people are already doing, there are adults from every generation and corner of society who haven't walked with their bare feet on Mother Earth or dug through soil with their bare hands with spiritual intention in decades, if ever. And there are kids of all ages that have never had the experience of directly connecting with nature beyond the playground at the neighborhood park or a few school field trips. This is serious, for there are serious physical, psychological, and spiritual issues, as well as significant societal repercussions, when people have little to no relationship with Mother Earth. A Medicine Walk is one of the highest forms of spiritual self-care that a human being can practice.

Although our indigenous ancestors didn't need medical studies or scientific research to understand the effects of our human relationship with nature, there are plenty of reports of the benefits, which include the following:

- Increased immune system performance
- Lowered blood pressure
- Increased blood flow throughout the body
- Reduced mental distraction and forgetfulness
- Improved focus, memory, and other core cognitive abilities
- Reduced hostile tendencies and quick-to-anger reactions
- Increased ability to work through stress, depression, and anxiety

Other benefits of a Medicine Walk that don't fit in the small and rigid box of modern-day colonized science are the powerful spiritual and psychic effects of our human connection with Mother Earth. A Medicine Walk brings increases in the following areas:

- Our intuition and other psychic senses
- The frequency and abilities in lucid dreaming
- Our ability to sense various natural energy fields
- Our ability to communicate with spirit guides and animals
- The effectiveness of connecting our prayer with action
- Our awareness of the natural earth medicine all around us
- Our ability to deflect negativity and attract positivity

Being on a Medicine Walk also allows us to disconnect from all the violence and negativity of the online world. When we devote our attention to the endless assault of people doing horrible things to each other and the horrific things we do to other sentient beings and to our planet, we disassociate from our morals and virtues, and our senses get dulled. Humans are not built to process the massive amount of pain, suffering, and cruelty we constantly expose ourselves to in the online world, which in turn creates many of the diseases in our heart, mind, and body. Unplugging from the online world and plugging in to nature is imperative to heal and regenerate our life force.

The Practice of a Medicine Walk

A Medicine Walk can be practiced anywhere that we can be in direct connection with nature. There's no need for an elaborate or dramatic display of ceremony in order to engage in the practice of a Medicine Walk, for this practice is intended to be a genuine, humble, and uncomplicated experience. To begin, set the intention for your walk, that it may be in the highest and best good in developing a sacred personal relationship with the healing powers and wisdom teachings of Mother Earth.

Next, slow down the flurry of your disconnected thought, and bring your consciousness back into your body by taking four slow and deliberate breaths deep into your heart space. The practice of a Medicine Walk requires a clear heart and clear mind in order to receive information with clarity. It may take a little while for your busy brain to adjust to the pace and vibration of the natural realm, so just do as many sets of four slow and deliberate breaths as it takes for your body and brain to ease into the present moment.

Next, greet the environment and introduce yourself. Offer a gift and ask to enter this sacred space while also stating your reason for being there, then give your thanks. For instance, "Beautiful Mother Earth, I offer you a gift of tobacco in a humble way and request to enter your sacred space and ask your help with discovering clarity and direction with a few issues I'm facing in my life. Mitákuye Oyás'iŋ; thank you." Keep it clear and simple, leave your offering, and begin your walk.

Practice using multiple senses to deliberately connect with the natural world around you. Then, at some point when it feels right, find a place to sit for a while and see what Mother Earth has to share with you. You can use as few or as many of the following methods as you want to help connect your consciousness with the message you're meant to receive from Mother Earth:

- Which way is the wind blowing? Is it coming in from the North, or is it blowing from the South? Which direction is the creek coming from and flowing to? Notice where the direction of nature is going to and coming from, because the lessons and wisdom these directions hold may help with things that are going out of or coming into your life, or with the answers or healings you're seeking.

- Many of us rely so heavily on our visual experience of the world that we've forgotten how to see without our eyes. Closing your eyes will heighten your other senses and enhance the world around you as you relearn how to see with your inner sight. Close your eyes and focus your hearing on the closest sounds you can hear and the farthest sounds you can hear. Once you've isolated a sound, imagine in detail what's going on to make that sound. Open your eyes, and find the sound you focused on. Maybe it's an ant dragging a moth back to the anthill or a grove of trees with their leaves quaking in the breeze. Observe all the details associated with the sound, and close your eyes again. Reimagine the scene and what's going on. By doing this, you're learning how to identify with and tune in to nature.

- Sit for a moment with your eyes closed and meditate with your prayer. Then open your eyes slowly, making sure not to focus on anything in particular. Allow your intuitive knowing and subtle sensory perceptions to guide your focus to whatever object draws your attention. Pick up that object, be it a feather, shell, pine cone, or leaf. Let's say it's a stone. Take your time and sit with the stone, imagine the life of that stone, and perhaps even ask it to take your worries from you. Energetically, put your worries into that stone, and then set it down directly on the earth or touching water, and let the soil or water take those worries and dissolve them into the earth. If you're putting prayers into something like a feather, then send your prayers up by placing the feather above the ground in a place where the sun can shine upon it during the day, the moon can shine upon it during the night, and the wind can swirl around it and carry your prayers to the farthest reaches of earth.

- If you want to connect with the spiritual entities of nature, such as little people and nature spirits, then you need to speak with them. Simply announce yourself and offer a gift—tobacco, food, or water. Do not introduce or leave anything unnatural in nature. Our spoken language may not be understood, but the energy in the tone of our voice will come across. Making a direct connection with nature spirits and entities can take a while, but when it happens, it can change your life forever because you learn that what you thought of as myths and legends are not fantasies. Consistency is key in making this connection, so you must continue to come back to the same place, placing your gifts in the same spot again and again. One day you just may notice a gift left in return! The relationship between a human and a nature entity is profoundly sacred and must be nurtured with the utmost honor and respect and with great secrecy to protect the being or beings.

- Leave the environment better than you found it. If you find trash, pack it out with you. Leave the place in a good way.

If conditions allow, stand with your bare feet on the ground. Release whatever you've been holding—anger, fear, shame, frustration, an argument, an overdue bill, an assignment that didn't get done. Relax your body and let it all dump out. Just let the earth take it. The earth is a filter and can transmute all the negative energetic toxins that you release into it.

And then, to receive, put your hands on the ground. If you're comfortable doing so, kneel down and put your forehead directly on the ground and say, "Please teach me." You don't have to say what needs to be taught, as the earth knows, and it will always give you what you need if you ask and give back in return.

And yes, by all means: hug a tree.

HÁU, MITÁKUYE OYÁS'IƝ

CHAPTER SIX

WANKÁTAKÁB– ABOVE

THE GREAT MYSTERY

*From Wakáŋ Tȟáŋka [Great Spirit] there came
a great unifying life force that flowed in and through all
things—the flowers of the plains, blowing winds, rocks,
trees, birds, animals—and was the same force that had
been breathed into the first man. Thus all things were
kindred and brought together by the same Great Mystery.*

— MATȞÓ NÁŽIŊ (CHIEF LUTHER STANDING BEAR)

The Great Mystery is the vital force that influences and inspires all that is within the sacred realm of Grandfather Sky—and so the very idea of defining the Great Mystery is somewhat absurd, because it doesn't matter how much we try to figure it out; we never will. We could gather the greatest living scientists, the most notable free-thinking philosophers, and the most enlightened spiritual gurus, and they'd never come to any understanding or conclusion on the Great Mystery. Given that, it's best to just enjoy being here, being human, and being in this moment, realizing that the bliss, beauty, and comprehension of the infinite cannot be known in this life, but that the answer to the Great Mystery will come—as it comes to us all—soon enough.

In the meantime, what we do know is that we are made of stardust. Basically, we're just water and stardust held together by a song from the universe. Each of us carries star medicine and whatever sacred force animates the stars also has a hand in our fate as Star Seeds. The Great Mystery may be incomprehensible but the ancestors tell us that it's in perfect harmony. If we attempt to live our lives according to worldly terms and human expectations instead of allowing our journey to unfold in flow with the Great Mystery, we will only be forcing needless suffering and struggle into our experience. Various indigenous cultures share some version of the teaching "The longest journey is the mind to the heart." It means that the behaviors of our human experiences here on earth are reflections of the movements of the celestial bodies above us. Consider, for example, the interrelationship between our higher conscious mind and our lower physical actions. There is a correspondence between above and below, a higher and a lower, and the ethereal and the earthly. Basically, it's a way to say that every action has an equal and opposite reaction and for every truth, there is an equal and opposite truth.

The Great Mystery is a neutral force that places no judgment or punishment on any sentient being. But because we humans fear the unknown and cannot understand the mystery of why things are happening the way they are, we label certain experiences as "good" or "bad" based on our very human perspectives and subjective experiences. When you label things, people, and experiences, you're only going to see what you've been conditioned to see, regardless of how open-minded you think you are. There are no good or bad experiences to reward or punish you, only those to teach you lessons that hopefully you explore and apply to your life.

ELEMENTAL ENERGY: BLOKÁ—MASCULINE

The sacred directions of Above and Below are intimately connected with the teachings of the symmetry of life. For not only does the celestial realm correspond with the earthly realm, but the primal elemental energies also share this relationship. The elemental energy associated with Above is Masculine. And the elemental energy associated with Below is Feminine.

The spiritual concept of masculinity has very little to do with being male. Certain concepts and beings, such as heaven, fire, hunting, and planting, are energetically rooted in the masculine. And certain concepts and beings, including earth, water, gathering, and harvesting, are energetically rooted in the feminine. Almost no concept or being is fully masculine or feminine all the time—sometimes we're connecting with our feminine energy and sometimes we're in connection with our masculine energy. Each of us has a natural resting point somewhere on the masculine-feminine scale.

In many indigenous cultures, the feminine energy is associated with creation and the masculine energy with functionality. For instance, females go through a very visceral rite of passage; a female's moon/menstrual cycle time is a monthly ceremony that spiritually purifies and cleanses her, preparing her for the potential of the creation of life. Males don't have a similar ritual, so they have to purify, cleanse, and prepare themselves spiritually in other ways.

That's why males go through certain purification ceremonies like sweat lodge and other rites of passage associated with manhood. The stages of manhood are like seeds that remain dormant until a set of conditions creates a catalyst moment that transitions one level of manhood to the next. But these rites of passage for males have all but disappeared in the modern world, deteriorating to something like getting the newest model of phone, playing the next version of a video game, or turning of age and going drinking. These are not spiritual rites of passage and they contribute nothing of substance to life.

Becoming a "man" has nothing to do with age or appearance. There are 40-year-old men who are boys and there are 16-year-old boys who are men. Being a man, or manhood, has to do with one's inherent sense of ultimate responsibility for oneself, the earth, and the living beings that reside on it.

Without rites of passage, many males find difficulty later in life relating to the concept of "I am a man." Many grown men have no idea what "being a man" is supposed to feel like and their disconnection from manhood is one of the most significant—and silent—factors contributing to the depression and struggle males experience in their lives.

Often, if a man lets his emotional guard down, other men often consider him a "sissy." If he takes morals and emotions into consideration instead of just logic, he's considered weak. If a man speaks up about the trauma that patriarchy and misogyny have caused women, then he's considered a traitor to the system of brotherhood that keeps men in power. If a male violates any of these unspoken rules of masculinity, other men often put him quickly in check and the pattern of behavior continues to march forward. The good news is that there are good men in this world working to change these behaviors.

What Are Men Missing?

For thousands of years, our youth had chores like feeding the animals, tending the soil, planting and harvesting, hunting and gathering, and other responsibilities that supported the life of the household and contributed to the community. In this modern age, our youth have little to no personal responsibilities that directly support, nurture, or protect their families or neighbors.

When a youth grows into adulthood without any responsibility to nurture, provide for, or protect their family, their community, or their natural surroundings, the disconnection from those responsibilities can manifest as being selfish, petty, apathetic, and judgmental. These adult males tend to be quick to anger and blame. Our modern world desperately needs men to heal from this ancestral trauma, as it's contributing to the worldwide pandemic of misogyny and patriarchy.

One key lesson to becoming a man is responsibility—specifically, developing the understanding from youth into adulthood that "I am ultimately responsible for myself." This does not mean being selfish or self-centered, but instead means that we are responsible for our life, as well as those things and people who are connected with our life. The way back to this understanding of ultimate responsibility begins with three behaviors:

1. **Providing**: I am responsible for providing for others and myself in a good way.

2. **Nurturing**: I am responsible for helping others and myself develop in a good way.

3. **Protecting**: I am responsible for the safety and well-being of others and myself in a good way.

When males don't feel responsible for these three principle behaviors, they will suffer from a lack of virility and vitality, and their inner light will become dim. For a male to Think Indigenous is for him to think in terms of providing, nurturing, and protecting himself, his village, and Mother Earth.

THE MEASURE OF A MAN

In the old days, when a young woman from a Northern Plains tribe was ready to marry, she would let her father know. Her husband would be hers to choose, but her father had to give his approval. For this to happen, the suitor would approach the father and let his intentions be known, and if he was an acceptable mate for the daughter, the father would give him a challenge.

The challenge the father set for the suitor may seem deceptively ordinary for that time in history and would have been something like "bring our family a buffalo" or "bring four horses from the Pawnee people." But hunting a buffalo or stealing horses from another nation of fierce warriors were life-threatening feats—and the ability to do these things had everything to do with how the man was raised, from boyhood into manhood.

In order to hunt a buffalo, the man would have had to learn from the other men in his village how to flint-knap an arrowhead. While it seems like a basic skill for that time, the man would have had to make thousands of arrowheads in order to learn to expertly craft an arrowhead that could penetrate the wooly fur and thick hide of a buffalo. And then there would have been the many years learning how to make the shaft of the arrow, how to prepare the wood to make the bow, how to craft the sinew for the string, and how to fletch the arrow with a specific type of feather for a specific type of animal; the hundreds of hunting trips taught by the best hunters from the camp; and the tens of thousands of shots made with the bow to be able to make the one shot when it would count the most. It meant experiencing the accidents that happened when hunting, surviving the unpredictable elements, and taking part in war parties going deep into enemy territory and counting coup. Not to mention all the stories, lessons, songs, skills, and wisdom that were learned while doing all these things over the many years of growing up.

The "simple" request of a buffalo or some horses was actually a profound test of courage, ability, and valor that allowed a father to decide if another man was worthy of marrying his daughter. If a man were capable of such a task, it meant that he had accomplished his rites of passages with honor and that he would be capable of providing for, nurturing, and protecting his family and community.

INDIGENOUS VIRTUES: OHÓLA NA YUÓNIHAŊ—RESPECT AND HONOR

The word *higher* refers to the spiritual energy of Above. It's why we use "higher" to signify certain concepts, such as higher meaning, higher power, higher self, higher knowledge, and so on. Many of these words are paired with the term *higher* to mark a distinct difference between the worldly meaning and the spiritual meaning. "Higher" refers directly to how we think of ourselves and how we think of others with regard to that spiritual place.

Respect and honor are associated with the sacred direction of Above because they run parallel to the power of our higher self, or self-respect.

Ohóla—Respect

Respect is the internal feeling we hold for someone or something when we admire them from afar for how they show up in the world. Respect is not given freely; it's earned. And much like integrity, it can take a long time to earn respect and an instant to lose it.

Self-respect is how we think about our self, how we talk to our self, how we nurture our body, how we follow our passions, how we ask for help when we need it, how we trust our intuition, and how we set and keep boundaries for our self. Self-respect is how we take responsibility for our life and know that we value and love our self.

All of our embarrassing little imperfections don't seem so imperfect when we have a powerful sense of self-respect. Having the courage and self-respect to simply *be who we are* is the best way we can show up and contribute to the world.

Yuónihaŋ—Honor

Honor is when we step out of our comfort zone and show someone or something else that we respect, love, and appreciate them for who they are or what they've done. One of the best and easiest ways to learn the lessons of honor is to express our feelings instead of just keeping them to ourselves. We honor our ancestors by setting out a Spirit Plate of food, we honor our loved ones by telling them the good things we notice about them and we can honor people we run across in our everyday life by letting them know that we respect them for who they are or what they've done.

When we express honor, we set off a powerful chain of events, for when others see us expressing honor, they may become inspired to do the same. It takes courage to honor someone or something, because it's hard to get past the dense energy of our self-consciousness and be vulnerable enough to express our feelings without any expectation of anything in return. But we're not striving for perfection. We're just progressing along our journey of higher self-actualization as part of our reverence for our life here on earth.

PERSONAL ASPECT: WÓOHOLA—REVERENCE

Reverence is what we do to show the spirit world we know it is there. It's common to hear people use the word *awe* when they talk about reverence, and that's probably because reverence inspires us to think beyond the self and acknowledge all that's on the other side of this world and this life. The act of spiritual reverence comes from all the virtues and morals on the medicine wheel: humbleness, humility, empathy, compassion, gratitude, generosity, honesty, integrity, and more.

We can show reverence for many things, including nature or a particular person, group, or time in history. And we must also have reverence for our ancestors on the other side. Your ancestors have your back. They help clear obstacles in front of you and send you clarity and help guide you with unseen hands.

One of the ways indigenous people honor their ancestors is by feeding them. When we eat, our ancestors eat with us. This way goes back thousands of years to nearly every indigenous tribe of people on every continent. When the Lakota people prepare food for their ancestors, it's called waéglepi—a Spirit Plate or Spirit Food. Spirit Food is endowed with the ability to maintain a quiet channel of communication for us with our ancestors and let the ancestors know they're invited into our home or gathering.

Anyone can practice this ancient way of giving reverence to our ancestors with Spirit Food. All you need to do is take a small, fork-sized amount of each food that you're eating and place it in a little bowl, on a plate, or even in a napkin. Pour a little water, coffee, or whatever you're drinking as well—a spoon-sized amount will do.

One day, we too will be ancestors.

The old ones tell us that our ancestors recognize this act of reverence because it lets them know we're thinking about them and that we know they're still with us. Remember that eventually our lives will end in this world and will pick back up on the other side. At that time, we'll be able to see our earth family from the other side and they'll be letting us know they know we're still with them when they set out a Spirit Plate for us.

SPIRITUAL PRACTICE:
IHÁŊBLA—SPIRIT DREAMING

Many indigenous cultures have an intimate relationship with the dream world. They purposefully work with their dreams as part of their everyday life to connect with the Great Mystery and the spirit realm. Many people seek out Native American spiritual leaders to help interpret their dreams because of the spiritual leaders' practice with lucid dreaming, or what the Lakota refer to as spirit dreaming. But spirit dreaming isn't something that's specific to the Lakota people—the dream world is available to anyone. Some people find meaning in their dreams and some dreams find the people who need meaning.

The ancestors tell us that spirit dreaming was one way our ancestors communicated with each other for thousands of years. It's how the medicine people of that time would send knowledge of the stars, transmit the design of pyramids, heal from a distance, or send warnings to each other. Any number of things that leave modern-day engineers, archaeologists, historians, and anthropologists scratching their heads in wonder and confusion can be attributed to the ancient ways of indigenous spirit dreaming.

Spirit dreaming isn't difficult, but like anything we want to become proficient in, it takes dedication and consistent practice. At one time or another, we've all probably had a powerful dream, such as one in which we're flying or doing something that seems so real we can't discern if we're in our perceived reality or the dream world. It's so amazing when it happens that we can't help but sit in awe of the phenomenal experience.

Now imagine if you could remain in that dream while also making conscious decisions and taking deliberate actions—that is a lucid dream. You can fly to a specific place instead of some random act of flying. Or you could have a meaningful back-and-forth discussion with someone instead of just fragments of incomprehensible phrases or activity. Or you could receive information directly from the spirit realm. Over time, you could increase your ability to intentionally dream to bring helpful information into our physical realm.

How to Begin Spirit Dreaming

Tonight, when you go to bed, repeat this to yourself: "I will remember that I'm dreaming." Keep focused on this phrase and don't let other thoughts come in to interrupt. Continue to repeat this in your mind as you fall asleep. This reminder to recognize that you're dreaming will subconsciously carry over into your dream state. As you drift into sleep and become aware that you're dreaming, you have to do something in your dream to test which reality you are in. For instance, you can pinch yourself. If you feel no pain, you'll know you're in the dream world. Once you're aware that you are in this dream state, you can intentionally explore your dreams and experiment with being unencumbered by physical laws. You can set any intention that you wish.

Practice, practice, practice! Just as with Rollerblading or ice-skating, you may not be that great the first or second time you try it, but once you get the hang of it, you'll wonder why everyone doesn't do this! While spirit dreaming, we can instruct the universe to clear any obstacles and protect us from any harm (both known and unknown) in our awake state. We can ask for clarity or for favor for our self, our family, and the beings of Mother Earth. We can ask to ease the suffering of those who are abused, diseased, affected by war, or oppressed. Then, with practice, when you're awake and you need a solution, you may just somehow know exactly what to do, as if the answer were just handed to you. Many times, you won't have to do anything, because the spirit world will have sent the energy necessary for the issue to work itself out without any effort on your part.

HÁU, MITÁKUYE OYÁS'IŊ

CHAPTER SEVEN

KHÚTA–BELOW

THE SOURCE OF LIFE

Mother Earth is the source of life, not a resource.
— CHIEF ARVOL LOOKING HORSE

⁝⁝⁝⁝⁝

The jungles and forests are the lungs of Grandmother Earth. The wind is moved by the ocean gyres and is the breath of Grandmother Earth. The creeks, rivers, and oceans are the vascular system of Grandmother Earth. The water that runs through them is the blood of Grandmother Earth. And the land under our feet is the flesh of Grandmother Earth. In every way that matters, the earth has its own physiology.

When we talk about the sacred direction of Below, we're referring to the teachings and indigenous medicines of Grandmother Earth that make up the source of all life. Grandmother Earth weaves the story of life on earth and the Creator provides the thread.

GRANDMOTHER EARTH

Our spiritual, nonphysical relationship and our living, physical relationship with earth are associated with Grandmother Earth. So, in the Lakota way, when we refer to either our Grandmother or our Mother, there's an unsaid understanding that we're honoring our sacred relationship with the earth.

Each of us is a unique child and a direct living descendant of Grandmother Earth. Each of us represents a living thread of humanity that's interwoven with the spiritual realm and the physical world of Grandmother Earth. All of us together, gathered under this understanding, make up this fabric of existence. We all share the same mother; we are all related, and we are all one nation.

ELEMENTAL ENERGY: YUWÍŊYAŊ S'E—FEMININE

Grandmother Earth represents the spiritual energy of the feminine and she holds the sacred spaces for the things that make us human. She holds space for where we pray and offer gratitude to the Creator, as well as the land where we grow our food and harvest our medicines. It's the benevolent feminine energy that nurtures the returning ones in the wombs of women and hallows the ground where we bury our loved ones when they go back home. Grandmother Earth blesses the ground where we hold our ceremonies and where we name our children and make each other relatives. She holds the medicine of the feminine for us to literally *live*.

The energy of the feminine is the spiritual womb that holds the life force of the earth and everything upon her. The power of the feminine is incalculable—and that's why the power structures of patriarchy have desperately done everything in their power to suppress the Truth of the Feminine for thousands of years. But the feminine is too powerful to be suppressed forever and we're now moving into the human era of masculine energy giving way to the energy of the feminine. It's not a moment too soon. The future is feminine.

We need to encourage and nurture the rise of the feminine power in gratitude for all the blessings the spiritual energy of the feminine has bestowed upon us. We do this by holding up our women, encouraging them to stand in their power, respecting their equal if not higher reasoning, reclaiming space for their energy and voice, and elevating them to the highest positions of power structures so they can rejuvenate our spiritually broken systems and processes. The salvation of humanity will be led by the power of the feminine.

WEAVING THE WORD

The Philippines is a country that is made up of more than 7,000 islands and multiple indigenous cultures. The Filipinos are world-renowned master weavers and their weaving invokes patterns and symbolism that represent their ancestors, folklore, nature-based spirituality, and various other aspects of their beautiful way of life.

In the old days, in some villages, the girls went through traditional rites of passage through the art of weaving. From a young age, the girl would sit with her mother as she harvested, scraped, rinsed, and beat plant material into fine fiber. And she would sit with other women in the village as they worked with the minerals from the earth and the tannins from the bark to make the dye for the yarn, and watch and learn as the intricate looms were set up. Throughout her life, the girl would be sent from aunties to grandmas to other women wisdom-keepers in the village to sit and talk and learn about the

77

> weaving, and these women would give great care and contemplation for when to share specific lessons and stories with the girl as she grew up.
>
> Through each stage in life, the girl would learn various ways of weaving fabric and other items, but one type of weaving would continue throughout her life: the art of weaving plant fiber into baskets. Basket weaving takes many years to master. It's said that when a girl becomes a young woman and she can weave plant fiber so fine that her baskets can hold water, it is then that she's ready to hold together a family.

INDIGENOUS VIRTUES: WÓWAČHAŊTOGNAKE NA OTÚȞ'AŊ— GENEROSITY AND RECIPROCITY

Wówačhaŋtognake—Generosity

The *meaning* of life is to discover our passions, and once they are discovered and developed, the *purpose* of life is to give our gift away. What comes to us naturally is our gift, a gift that we have probably practiced over many lifetimes. We "give our gift away" by integrating that gift with how we walk in this world and how we support ourselves—not just financially, but also by how we support our spirits and our walk on the Red Road.

On the Red Road, when we give something away, we never feel that anything is owed back. Ownership of things is not a concept we understand—even ownership of ideas and knowledge. In Western culture, when somebody has an idea, it belongs to that person—it's patented, copyrighted; it's theirs. But in indigenous cultures, we put our heads together and share ideas and if someone takes an idea and runs with it, that's borrowing, not thievery—for there is no ownership of the idea. The thinking is, that idea is not mine; I'm just the person it happened to come through. Someone else can borrow it, but they can't own it—and neither can I. This kind of generosity, which doesn't include a concept of ownership, could make the world a different place. But it does require self-care. Being generous is good, but being generous should not result in the suffering of our own health, happiness, or well-being. We must remember not to be martyrs. We must be generous with ourselves first, which starts with being generous with our spirits. Otherwise, it's only a matter of time before our spirit will rise up to express itself, and we may not be in a stage of life or have the ability to reconcile the needs of our spirit. That's when life can get rough.

Otúȟaŋ—Reciprocity

Reciprocity is like an echo. Whatever we put out into the world will come back to us multiplied—which is why reciprocity is both the primary cause of our personal suffering and the secret to abundance. With the right relationships in the right environment, the reciprocal exchange of spiritual energy can grow exponentially until a truly amazing phenomenon occurs: a state of divine equilibrium. This happens when spiritual energy is nurturing and growing itself in a complete circuit and it is another example of the Sacred Hoop of Life.

At Standing Rock, during the months-long protest of the Dakota Access Pipeline, there was a pile of wood the size of a small house. As the year grew colder and so many of us were trying to keep warm, you would expect that pile of wood to deplete. But there was a sign next to the pile of wood, reminding us of reciprocity: "Chop three, take two." And in this way of living in a community, there was always more than enough wood for everyone who needed it. There were people at Standing Rock from all over the world and one simple sign created a way of doing things that reverberated throughout all the camps in various ways, where everyone got their needs met and there was always enough.

THE THREE SISTERS

One of the oldest stories on Turtle Island is the tale of the three sisters: Corn, Beans, and Squash. The oldest sister is tall and strong, with graceful green leaves and wisps of golden, silky hair that flow out of her wrapped fruit. Her name is Corn. The middle sister is wild and vivacious, with curly vines that climb up and around her sister, Corn, which helps make Corn steadfast in the wind and protected from the elements. Her name is Beans. The little sister is curious and playful, quickly crawling and exploring all over the ground. She has wide leaves and loves to make people smile by showing them her happy yellow flower blossoms. Her name is Squash.

The three sisters love each other in that magical way that only sisters understand. When planted together, their lives are intertwined in ways that reciprocate the love they share for one another—and the abundance of that sisterhood benefits the world around them. Sister Corn not only provides fruit and grain but offers her sturdy form for Sister Beans to climb up and reach the sun that she needs to grow her ample fruit to feed the people of the land. The roots of Sister Beans offer nitrogen to the soil below, and her tendrils stabilize Sister Corn above the ground. Their little sister, Sister Squash, grows at the feet of Sister Corn and Sister Beans, where she shades the ground with her broad leaves to help hold moisture in the soil and protect against the aggressive weeds. The bounty of their harvest provides the indigenous people with necessary energy, protein, vitamins, and minerals.

The Three Sisters teach us the power of reciprocating love in the most grounded way possible.

PERSONAL ASPECT: WAKȞÁŊ—THE SACRED

How do we know when something is wakȟáŋ or sacred? In Native American spirituality, if everything is interconnected, then wouldn't it make sense that every single thing on Mother Earth is sacred?

In fact, yes. We two-legged must understand our intimate connection between landscape and spirituality. This understanding is at the center of indigenous societies. We believe in a universe where supernatural beings exist within the same time and space as humans and our natural world. The sacred places simultaneously exist in both as visible and invisible realities. That is, they live unseen, but known, within a physical place visible to indigenous people.

One such place for Lakota people and many indigenous nations is Matȟó Pahá—Bear Butte, South Dakota. This mountain is a sacred place.

To the Lakota, Bear Butte has long been a place to hold council meetings and ceremonies such as vision quests and Sun dances. In the mid-1800s the father of Crazy Horse, a great holy man, climbed Bear Butte to seek spiritual guidance on a vision quest.

It has been said that Wakȟáŋ Tȟáŋka appeared before the holy man in the form of a bear and gave him power to overcome obstacles and defeat his enemies. Crazy Horse's father asked that the same gifts also be given to his son. After this bestowment, the mountain was known as Bear Butte, or Mata Paha.

The history of Bear Butte is rich, as well as literal; artifacts dating back 10,000 years have been discovered near it. Tipi rings have been found along Bear Butte's perimeter, in addition to rocks, or clarions, the Lakota placed along the mountain's summit to mark distances and to offer prayers. Many note a profound spiritual connection when visiting the site.

Indigenous people speak of how this mountain is a liminal space, a place between two realms.

We can go near this sacred place to perceive the divine, but we believe that changing the physical landscape in these places disrupts Grandmother Earth. We view this as a desecration.

Everything that is natural is sacred; it just takes emerging from the fog of our limited human belief system to comprehend it. The concept of wakȟáŋ—or the sacred—does not in any way have a religious meaning. It supersedes all religion, as it is the embodiment of the original truth and design of all that is.

Honor the Sacred

Now. It is here
Look around
The disease of taking is destruction in making
Please no more faking, we are awakening
Quite literally cancer, exploitation is not the answer
Everything is not okay, no matter what the box says
This is not how it has to be
Not how it has been
Certainly not what will be

Everything connected
Taking from life is taking from all life
Your life. My life. Our life
Taking with no giving is killing
Reciprocation honors all creation
One Nation. All Nations
Reconcili-action can heal every faction

Respect
Where we intersect
All the way down to the littlest insect, honor all flesh
Every story lived faces death
Cherish each breath
Still there is hope left
Love happens, healing happens, miracles happen
This much we know
This is our journey
Each of us the hero. The miracle. The center of change. The
center of choice
My (our) next choice is the choice our ancestors told stories of
What I (we) choose in this present moment is everything
Are we (I) choosing to tend the garden of LIFE?

Come together through LIFE
or come together through death
We are always together
Remember
Everything else is illusion
Born from the Mother, return to the Mother
No fear
Great Spirit dances in cycles
Birth and death meeting at every point
Every moment. Full circle
Balance will be restored

— Unity Sferrazza

SPIRITUAL PRACTICE:
WAKȞÁŊ OKÓ—SACRED SPACES

There are two sacred spaces that are important in keeping
us spiritually grounded: our indoor spaces and our outdoor

spaces. This can also refer to our subconscious and conscious. While it's easy for us to appreciate the breathtaking beauty of Mother Earth's unblemished natural landscapes, we often pay little attention to our indoor environments, which are where we spend most of our lives. Even though we spend most of our time inside, we tend to have very unhealthy indoor spaces. Far too many architects over the last several decades have designed our living spaces with no understanding of how energy moves, let alone how our home spaces need to be sacred places. There are exceptions, such as Frank Lloyd Wright's masterpiece, Fallingwater, which is a brilliant integration of indoors and outdoors in a home. But most architects merely design our spaces to be minimally functional. Even high-end homes may have more square footage, higher ceilings, and better appliances, but they're certainly not given spiritual consideration. Simply putting a big Buddha-head statue in the foyer of a mansion doesn't make the inhabitants spiritual, nor does it make the space sacred.

However, the indigenous peoples have understood the spiritual energy of our indoor and outdoor spaces for thousands of years. The study and practice of spiritually harmonizing people with their indoor and outdoor environments is an ancient practice taught by Grandmother Earth with sacred geometry. Indigenous cultures all over the world have listened to the earth for guidance on how to build their homes and how to dress.

The Lakota people in the plains built teepees, easy to build and take down to allow for nomadic hunting, and the Alaskan people built homes with ice and snow, allowing them to withstand the long cold winters. All these homes are round to allow for energy to flow freely and because where there are no corners, there is nowhere to hide.

It would be impractical to cover the immense and detailed understanding of indigenous buildings in this short section about the spiritual practice of sacred spaces, but the similarities between all indigenous principles of building and indigenous Native American spirituality are striking. All are based on four principles: Energy Flow, Natural Elements, Grounding Elements, and Healing Acceptance.

Energy flow is the universal energy that moves all things seen and unseen, the same energy that Natives call Spirit or Sacred Movement—takú wakȟáŋ škaŋškáŋyaŋ. There's an interesting similarity between the Native American medicine wheel and the Bagua in that the Bagua is an eight-sided shape that represents the energy map of the primary principles of feng shui, and the medicine wheel is a circular energy map of the primary principles of indigenous Native spirituality, including the Sacred Hoop of Life. There's also vastu shastra, an indigenous Indian practice that's thought to predate feng shui by at least a thousand years. In fact, many indigenous cultures all over the earth have long known of the spiritual energy that's shared between us humans and our sacred spaces.

The idea of this practice of spiritually reconnecting with our personal spaces is simple. All it requires is finding small ways to bring nature indoors and get us back out in nature. The power of our private sanctuary—our home—can help us let go of the expectations and pressures that were placed onto our shoulders by the outside world so we can ground our self and heal our unseen wounds.

To begin, let's get creative and imagine all the ways we can bring nature back into our sacred spaces based on our senses of sight, smell, hearing, taste, and touch, as well as our psychic senses. Keep in mind that each of us has a unique spiritual journey, so we will each have a different sacred space.

WaŋyáŋkA—Sight

When it's time to update your artwork—and, let's be honest, it's probably time—choose artwork with nature-based themes and natural materials that makes you feel relaxed, calm, and happy. The same goes for things in your home, such as furniture and anything to do with home and outdoor décor, including paint, wallpaper, tile, and landscape design choices. Begin to notice the lighting you have around your home. Lighting can improve the mood and atmosphere, and it can also decrease eye fatigue and headaches. Open those curtains and let in the sun! Let your eyes rest upon things that are beautiful.

Mná—Smell

The smell of pine after a summer rain, the smell of a wet dog shaking off after jumping in the lake, or the smell of a campfire—these are all powerful enough to evoke even the most remote memories. Aromas can wake up our senses, enliven us, and bring a heightened sense of awareness to our environment. We can add beautiful aromas to our homes every now and then to create another layer of ambience to our sanctuary by crushing some lavender, burning some sweetgrass, cleansing our space by burning a little sage, or burning some cedar when we pray. We can use smell to lift ourselves up into a higher mood of tranquility and positive energy.

Naȟ'úŋ—Hearing

Is the wind blowing, are the birds singing, or is there thunder rolling in from the distance? Open your windows! It may seem obvious to bring in beautiful sounds or music to better our space and mood, but often our sense of hearing is something we take for granted. We forget to close our eyes and *listen* to all that's going on in the space around us. The opposite is also true; if there's traffic or construction or other human-made noise, make efforts to block that noise or seek silence. The key to the sense of hearing is to combine it with other senses. Good music in a room with perfect lighting and a scented candle or having the windows open while we work on a passion project can be amazing for self-care.

Yul-íyuthA—Taste

Our sense of taste is important, because it's directly tied to both our emotions and our nervous system. The flavors of sweet, sour, salty, bitter, savory, and umami all have the ability to instantly change our mood and lift our spirits. We can enhance our experience when we create a dish that matches the mood we want and take it outside to eat. We can do the same with a favorite beverage. The idea is for us to understand that food is medicine. Refreshments are served at gatherings to bless our guests with refreshing energy and replenish the body with life. Going outside and enjoying our life-giving food bite by bite instead of mindlessly eating in front of the TV or scrolling through our mobile devices will help replenish the body and the spirit.

Épathaŋ—Touch

Our sense of touch is ruled by pain or pleasure and nearly every part of our body can feel this sense. Use your sense of touch to experience pleasure with those things you come in physical contact with, which can be simple, everyday items that we take for granted. It could be the cup you use for coffee or tea, or the handles or knobs on your doors and drawers, or the razor in the bathroom. You can upgrade the objects you touch in your house every day and make the world a better place while you're at it! Use bamboo- or wood-handled dish scrubbers and kitchen utensils instead of plastic ones. Invest in a safety razor and stop throwing plastic razors and cartridges into the environment. Begin to do more things by hand rather than using modern-world conveniences. Touch your food to prepare it instead of just dumping it out of a can into a bowl and microwaving it. It's healing to work with your food by making it from fresh ingredients, to touch it, to bless it, and to infuse your love into it. Cooking and cleaning can be therapeutic, meditative, fulfilling, and even fun when done with heartfelt intention.

Nağíksab'ič'ila AblézA—Psychic Senses

We should never underestimate how much unseen energy affects us. When we share space with sentient beings, we're also sharing their natural energy and this natural and unseen energy plays a role in our healing and self-actualization in ways we may not even realize. Our sacred spaces are vessels for love and we need to feed and nurture that love. We can do this by taking the time to walk the dog or lay with the cat. We can bring real plants into our home instead of fake plastic ones. We can grow our own herbs and medicines.

Not only can our home be a natural incubator in the development of our psychic senses but sharing our lives with sentient beings that we nurture and love helps the negative fall away just by inviting them into our home. When we do many little things with great intention, across a wide range of our senses, they compound and amplify the energy and greatly harmonize our sacred spaces.

HÁU, MITÁKUYE OYÁS'IŊ

CHAPTER EIGHT

HÓČHOKA–CENTER

THE CENTER OF LIFE

*I salute the light within your eyes where
the whole Universe dwells.
For when you are at that center within you
and I am that place within me,
we shall be one.*

— Tȟašúŋke Witkó, (Crazy Horse)

When Crazy Horse said, "I salute the light within your eyes where the whole Universe dwells," he was describing the moment when two spiritually connected beings recognize each other, as if they've known each other a thousand years, even though they may have just met.

Each of us is but a doorway through which the Creator expresses Itself in our particular physical image at this particular moment in the cosmic workings of the Great Mystery. When we meet each other for the first time, we are either about to repeat a pattern or recurring theme in our life, or we're about to experience some type of new beginning. The light in our eyes—when we learn to recognize it—tells us the difference between the two.

As we learn to connect with the ways of the medicine wheel and our natural sense of spirituality, we realize that we're not separate from nature—we are nature itself. We're sentient beings that are naturally synchronized with the cycles of the sun, the moon, the stars, and the seasons of the land on which we live. Think about the power of nature. Consider the moon—something of such great influence that it can pull and push the all-powerful oceans of the world in both tide and current. And then consider: How can we believe the moon has no effect on us humans, even though we are mostly created from and composed of water? The fact is the moon greatly affects us, but many people have become too desensitized to feel her affects. Tuning back in to these types of natural energies takes practice.

We are not separate from the Hoop and we are not at the top of the food chain, as humans like to think, but we are part of the whole. When we say Mitákuye Oyás'iŋ, or "We are all related," it doesn't mean that only we two-legged humans are related, but that we are *all* related—every single sentient being on the matrix of Grandmother Earth. When we brush a single strand of the spider's web, that energy is transmitted and felt on every strand and connection point throughout the rest of the web. The indigenous tribes of the Amazon have a popular fable that teaches about the web of life, in which a butterfly flapping its wings in the jungle stirs the wind that creates many more small wind currents that divide and multiply and ultimately manifest into a hurricane on the other side of the world a few days later. The teaching is that *all* is connected, and our daily actions are inextricably braided into *everything else* in ways that we may never fully comprehend in the present moment.

The power structures of our modern-day society distract us from our internal understanding that we are part of that *all*. On every part of the earth, we can clearly see the devastation and horror humans inflict on other sentient beings and the destruction we bring to Grandmother Earth. It's not just the bad medicine humans bring to the world, but it's also the disrespect and abuse we inflict on ourselves mentally, physically, and spiritually with the toxic waste that we allow into our hearts, minds, and bodies. For those of us that walk the Red Road, it's part of our life's work to dismantle these harmful power structures in all the ways that we're able to.

There will come a time in each of our lives when we have to be honest with ourselves and decide if we're going to live in alignment with Grandmother Earth or live for a corporate system. This may be the most important decision we face in this lifetime—because finding our Center and living a life of genuine meaning and beauty is what's at stake.

ELEMENTAL ENERGY: WIČHÓNI—LIFE

The Four Sacred Elements, the Seven Sacred Directions, and the Seven Indigenous Values are all concepts to help us think indigenously and understand the natural order of the earth and the fundamentals of indigenous spirituality. It's in the Center of our being where we take these concepts and implement them into the experience of our daily lives.

Too often, however, we become so absorbed in the memories of our past and so fearful of the what-if scenarios of the future that we miss the experience of the present moment. When we learn to drop into the experience of the present moment, we become aware and available to the power and teachings of the sacred directions that are moving through us.

When we talk about the Center, we're referring to our life. Our life is the space through which the other six sacred directions are moving at all times. The innermost point of the Center is where we experience the present moment—and it's within the present moment that we're consciously co-creating our life as part of the wild divine. This space is also where we step away from our work-eat-disengage-sleep cycle and go deeper into the understanding of life and our role as a human being on this earth.

INDIGENOUS VIRTUES: WÓWIYUŠKIŊ, THEȞÍLA, HAHÁYELA NA WÓKSAPE—JOY, LOVE, HARMONY, AND WISDOM

Joy, love, harmony, and wisdom are the four primal expressions of our spirit through which we discover who and what we truly are and the teachings of how we are meant to engage life. The four sacred directions of East, South, West, and North each carry one of these four expressions as they move through our Center.

Wiyóhiŋyaŋpata—East: Haháyela—Harmony

We're starting the teachings of the four expressions with harmony because, when the other expressions of joy, love, and wisdom are in balance in our lives, their harmony becomes the bedrock of our spiritual intelligence.

Harmony is the combined state of tranquility, unity, and readiness between our thoughts, well-being, spirituality, and physiology. Harmony is not the pursuit of perfection in these areas of our life but the awareness and development of our internal relationship with them, as well as how we extend that spirit energy out into the world. Remember, we are meant to be human—we are not meant to be perfect. Harmony is not a state of perfection but a state of awareness of balance.

We are often our own biggest obstacle in experiencing genuine harmony in our life. As perfectly imperfect humans, we easily get stuck thinking in terms of who or what we need to control, or who or what we need to exploit for our personal gain, or how we want others to see us. Observing is the secret to allowing oneself the ability of letting go of these unhelpful and hollow desires. The Sacred Hoop of Life already has natural cycles that we can observe just by intentionally connecting with nature and doing so helps us merge into the powerful rhythm of life itself.

Allowing is just getting out of our own way and allowing the rhythm of life to help co-create our life with us. The Creator is more clever and creative than we could ever be and allowing the Creator to just go forth and create will bring results and experiences we never could have imagined or created by pursuing them with our human desire for control, personal gain, or ego satisfaction.

Itókaǧata—South: Wóksape—Wisdom

What is wisdom and where does it come from? Simply put, wisdom is experience in action. The old ones tell us that teachings from the spirit world travel on the wind and the wind is born in the South. That is why the sacred direction of the South carries the spiritual teachings of wisdom.

> *Listen to the Earth. It speaks.*
> *Listen to the Fire. It speaks.*
> *Listen to the Wind. It speaks.*
> *Listen to the Water. It speaks.*
> *Listen to your Heart. It knows.*
>
> *— The Ancestors*

Geronimo, a Chiricahua Apache leader and medicine man, said that wisdom and peace begin when we start living the life the Creator intended for us. But we don't have to live in a cave for 30 years contemplating our navel to achieve some sort of enlightened wisdom. And the unabridged, esoteric wisdom of the universe certainly won't come flooding into our consciousness after one sweat lodge ceremony. Wisdom begins to unfold as we accumulate the experiences of living our life in alignment with the natural laws of the universe and how and when we put those teachings from our life into motion. Whether we are consciously aware of it or not, everything we experience in our life is both offering us what we're here to learn in this life (what we need) and preparing us for what we're praying for in our life (what we want).

If you recall, the sacred element of the South is air. When air expresses itself, it comes as the unseen force of wind. Wind is associated with wisdom, because the nature of wind is to bring messages, initiate change, animate life, and bring clarity by removing obstacles and clearing obstructions. When the obstacles and obstructions are removed from our mind, we can understand things better because of that clarity. It's this type of clarity that cultivates wisdom.

Walking with Wisdom

Wisdom is the part of spiritual intelligence that allows us to see people and situations with clarity, as well as a natural understanding of the relationship between seemingly unrelated things.

Being wise has a lot to do with knowing what *not* to do, like knowing when to pause instead of taking action, or knowing when to praise instead of being critical, or knowing when to listen instead of talking. For example, when you communicate with an indigenous elder, you may notice they speak deliberately and may take long pauses between thoughts before they reply to your question. They are allowing their information to be heard and thought through and for the intention of the message to blossom in its own space. In most conversations in modern society, many of us aren't truly listening as much as we're just waiting for the slightest pause so we can jump in and speak to fill the void.

We must be mindful that a pause is not an invitation to give feedback if feedback was not asked for. Understanding the pause in a conversation is the difference between talking "at" someone and talking "with" someone. Practice pausing before you speak. When you do speak, evaluate if what you have to contribute is even relevant and beneficial to what's already been said or what is already understood. The old ones teach us that our tongue is connected to our heart— the lesson being for us to learn to speak through our heart rather than letting whatever comes into our brain go running straight out of our mouth. Our breath carries power— our words can provide clarity, our words can heal, and our words can destroy—so let's not be reckless or wasteful with the wisdom of our words.

To be wise is to be relational. When it's time to offer advice, don't give direct advice, but instead offer something relational so that those listening can arrive at their own conclusions. Many times, the person you're advising already knows what to do; they're just looking for permission to do it. We cannot give them that permission—that permission must come from within themselves, through free will. Wisdom has a lot to do with guiding people to their own conclusion rather than leading them to *your* answer.

Always look to your heart to stay truthful.

—Doug Good Feather

Wiyóȟpeyata—West: Wówiyuškiŋ—Joy

Joy is what elevates us into the best that life has to offer. Life is not meant to be easy—in fact, at times, life is meant to be difficult and the very act of living and engaging in life comes with trials and tribulations that can pull us into the undercurrent of an ocean. But joy is what pulls us out of that depression or suffering and prevents us from getting swept out to sea.

We can start by finding a buoyant sense of joy. With a buoy in an ocean, it doesn't matter if the sea is calm or raging, because the buoy's natural resting state is unsinkable. When we stop struggling, it's our natural state to float—both in the ocean and in life. A buoyant sense of joy may even save your life at those times when everything feels impossible.

Living a Joyful Life

Finding what gives us joy may be as simple as making a list of the things that make us happy, another list of what we do most every day, and then comparing the two lists and adjusting accordingly to bring in more of what gives joy and let go of what doesn't. We can also integrate joy into even the most mundane activities in our daily life. Finding joy *is* simple and it grows easier with practice.

The underlying causes for our loss of joy—whether that loss is temporary or long-term—are often our judgments and expectations about people or situations. A judgment refers to what we perceive to be true and an expectation refers to our assumption of future results. When we prejudge something, we don't allow for the possibilities of anything else and we block out any potential to find the interesting idiosyncrasies or serendipity the universe has to offer us. There is joy in the mystery of the unknown. And when we have preset expectations of how something needs to be, most often we are just setting ourselves up for disappointment.

How can we predict what's going to happen in the future? Disappointment robs us of joy, so releasing our expectations of how something needs to be or happen allows us to appreciate how the Creator offers up what we honestly need and not necessarily what we merely want.

In most situations, our buoyant sense of joy won't be at risk when we do things without the expectation of anything in return. The biggest thief of joy in our modern world is the epidemic of comparing ourselves to others, not only because it robs us of our joy but also because we have absolutely no idea what someone else's personal journey is all about. When we desire the lives of others, we may energetically bring all *their* hard-learned lessons over into our lives, without getting any of the benefits that we think they have. As the saying goes, be careful what you wish for.

The thing is, it's extremely likely that you have far more joy in your life than you realize, but you just can't get to it because it's been covered up by traumas that you've experienced. Healing these energetic traumas may reveal the joy that's been there all along. It's important to remember that all in-depth healing cannot be truly complete until it's reconciled through spiritual connection. Otherwise the trauma will continue to come up again and again and may even show up in the physical world as a disease or psychiatric disorder. Healing comes from within us. Medicine people, doctors, and traditional practitioners can only help us redirect and focus our energy to facilitate our health and healing and a buoyant sense of joy is the fulcrum for deep spiritual healing.

Wazíyata—North: Theȟíla—Love

What is love but the life force for all of life? Let's consider how dimly or brightly love shines through us in our personal life. What does it mean when we talk about love shining through us? It means that love is one of the four primal spiritual expressions of our spirit, because it's an accumulation of how we radiate joy, how we embody wisdom, and how we foster harmony in the various ways we show up in life. Love is expressed in how we show our love to others, how we let love in from others, and how we understand and spiritually process and work with love as it matures and evolves.

The person you will spend the most time with in your life is *you*, and that's why it's of utmost importance that you learn to care for, accept, and love yourself first and foremost. It's much more difficult than it sounds, because we're often our own worst critic, bully, and abuser. If we want to be loved—both by ourselves and others—we must make ourselves lovable. And we become lovable when we heal the parts of ourselves that we're ashamed of or that we think are embarrassing or unlovable.

Essentially, we must learn to love the many things about ourselves that we think are unlovable, including our emotional weaknesses and physical imperfections, our torrid and shameful past, and our lack of self-confidence and self-worth. When we haven't healed and we don't love ourselves first, we abuse those we are supposed to protect, betraying that which we are supposed to defend. We damage those we are supposed to love and we hurt those we are supposed to heal. Hurt people inadvertently hurt people. Through the indigenous ways of natural spirituality and walking the Red Road, we can find our way back to love through the healing of our invisible moral injuries and trauma.

SPIRITUAL PRACTICE: THE REFLECTION

This practice requires you to be vulnerable. It asks you to find all the love for yourself that you can.

Stand naked in front of a mirror and look. Really see yourself. Notice what your mind does—you probably look at all that is negative about yourself, all that you don't like. This is what the modern world has conditioned us to think about ourselves—we are trained to only see the worst, to judge and to compete.

What is that you see? Are you judging yourself for your weight, wrinkles, imperfect skin, or scars? Allow yourself to see all that you judge and view it as honestly as you can.

Now force yourself to move to the positive. This won't be easy at first, as it is not what we are trained to do. Again, we have been conditioned to look only at the negative in ourselves. There are so many positives and they far outnumber the negatives, but they can be hard to see.

Perhaps you can look at your hands and notice that they are your father's hands—capable hands.

Perhaps you can look at your wrinkles, wrinkles that you dislike, but can remember a beloved photograph of a grandmother whose wrinkles you love because of how beautifully worn she is in life. Can you find the evidence of your own wisdom and good life? Can you find smile lines and appreciate that a face without smile lines would in fact be tragic?

Perhaps you can look at your strong legs and feet and remember how dependable they are, how far they have carried you and will continue to carry you.

Eventually, this practice will make you feel empowered more than vulnerable. You will truly see yourself, in the negative and the positive. You will find love for all of yourself.

HÁU, MITÁKUYE OYÁS'IŊ

CHAPTER NINE

THE
THREEFOLD PATH

The Seven Sacred Directions have taught us how to *think* indigenous. But how do we *live* indigenous? We have found three related pathways to living a modern life while also maintaining this nature-based spirituality:

- **The Way of the Seven Generations:** *Conscious living* is a modern term for the ancient way of living in harmony with the laws of nature and making decisions based on how our choices will affect the lives of our unborn relatives seven generations from today. It also takes into account the many generations that have come before us, who stand as examples of what to do and what not to do, so that we learn from past mistakes and successes.

- **The Way of the Buffalo:** *Mindful consumption* is a modern term for the ancient practice of respecting and honoring all beings on Mother Earth. This practice requires being intentional and deliberate with our stewardship of the land

and learning how to live within a circular, aware mindset.

- **The Way of the Village:** *Collective impact* describes the process of finding your community, being a part of an indigenous-thinking community, and elevating planetary consciousness when we work, play, and pray together.

THE WAY OF THE SEVEN GENERATIONS

I see a time of Seven Generations when all the colors of mankind will gather under the Sacred Tree of Life and the whole Earth will become one circle again.

— TȞAŠÚŊKE WITKÓ, (CRAZY HORSE)

Crazy Horse, a venerated Lakota warrior, was shown a powerful vision that there would be a time of Seven Generations, when all the colors of humankind would gather under the Tree of Life and Grandmother Earth would welcome the hearts and minds of the spiritually disconnected back into the ways of her mysterious knowledge. At that time, there would be indigenous wisdom keepers that carry knowledge and understanding of unity among all living things and others would come to listen and learn the ways of indigenous wisdom. The teachings tell us that humanity has arrived at this era of awakening and connection.

The old ones say that we do not inherit the earth from our ancestors but that we borrow it from our children. To live life according to the Way of the Seven Generations means to think and act in such a way that each of our decisions and actions is made with the deep consideration and wisdom of our ancestral past, our eventual impact on Mother Earth, and the future lives of the unborn. The seven generations include both the seven generations that preceded our life and the seven generations that have yet to come. By taking the time to learn from the generations upon generations of our previous ancestors, we can bypass common mistakes and experience success and happiness more quickly and more often. There's an ancient proverb that says, "All the flowers, of all the tomorrows, are in the seeds of today." This is just another example that indigenous cultures from all parts of the world—not just Native Americans—knew the way of the seven generations thousands of years ago. And as the ancestors know, thousands of years is not a long time, whether we're going back in history or forward into our future.

MITÁKUYE OYÁS'IŊ—WE ARE ALL RELATED

A grandfather takes his grandchild out to fish for the first time; a grandmother and auntie take a child out to gather berries and wild foods. In this way we teach our children the value of caring, compassion, and the indigenous way of living. The first time a child is taught to fish or gather berries, nuts, or roots, that food is always given away to other members of the family in a special ceremonial meal. Everyone is invited to the feast and shares in the food gathered by the child, except the guest of honor, the child. The child is pleased because they are able to provide for the family in a powerful way and gets to enjoy the bounty of the hard work with all the people they love. The child does not go hungry but they cannot eat any of the food they gathered or caught at the ceremonial feast. This first meal provided by the child's first hunt, fishing trip, or gathering with the grandmothers honors the community and the child. Sharing is a way of life for the indigenous

> people. No one can survive on their own. We are all related, and as such we are all responsible for each other. This responsibility creates conscious living practices.
>
> HÁU MITÁKUYE OYÁS'IŊ

Conscious Living

Conscious living is a modern way of considering how the decisions we make today will impact the next seven generations. For life to continue to move forward, we must teach our children early in their lives what we adults have collectively learned later in our lives. This is how the belief system of a collective consciousness evolves in a good way.

This is not to say it's easy. In this modern world, it can be hard to feel like you are living in alignment with your beliefs. We all have to buy food, we all have to get from place to place, we all have to pay bills and sometimes those needs and responsibilities demand that we compromise our beliefs. Eating toxic food, driving fossil-fueled vehicles, going to a job that is meaningless—or worse yet, that is harmful or destructive to other beings and the environment—are all things that we may do that don't support our belief systems. This can be hard to accept, but we aren't in this time and place just so we can lose hope. Fear and despair may be contagious, but so is hope and courage. We shouldn't have to live in a world where it's up to us to protect our health and the environment from politicians and corporations, but that's the world we live in. *We* are the ones we've been waiting for, and we need to understand that we are the guardians of the earth and we must integrate this realization into our lives as best we can and as soon as we can. All of the spiritual awakening in the world won't help the earth or humanity if we don't live what we learn.

Living in Harmony with Mother Earth

The pollution of Mother Earth is simply the external reflection of our inner spiritual relationship with the Creator or, in other words, our self. When millions and millions of us are spiritually disconnected from ourselves—not living in alignment with the ways of Mother Earth or the natural laws of the universe—then it's easy to see how we as a society can defile this earth without much consideration of the results of our actions and decisions.

> *I used to think that top environmental problems were biodiversity loss, ecosystem collapse, and climate change. I thought that 30 years of good science could address these problems. I was wrong. The top environmental problems are selfishness, greed, and apathy, and to deal with these, we need a cultural and spiritual transformation. And we scientists don't know how to do that.*
>
> — GUS SPETH, COFOUNDER OF THE NATURAL RESOURCES DEFENSE COUNCIL AND FORMER DEAN OF YALE SCHOOL OF FORESTRY AND ENVIRONMENTAL STUDIES

The first lesson of living in harmony with Grandmother Earth is learning the acts of self-care and self-actualization. We can't expect to live in harmony with Grandmother Earth if we're not in harmony with ourselves—and we can't expect to see changes in this world if we're not making changes within. All change begins with the self. Harmony does not happen just because we suddenly choose to be in harmony with something or someone else; harmony begins when we begin to *work* on that harmony.

> *To heal the land, we must heal each other.*
> *But to heal each other, we must first heal ourselves.*
> — DOUG GOOD FEATHER

Do you want to change the world? Well, loving your-self is the first and highest form of direct action. Imagine how many corrupt people would lose power and how many greedy corporations would collapse if we all simply decided that we loved ourselves. If we loved our bodies, we wouldn't poison them with toxic food. We wouldn't drink water out of plastic bottles—water that's being stolen by evil corpo-rations. If we loved our self, we wouldn't let the military industrial complex manufacture wars for their profit. And we wouldn't let the oil and gas extraction industry continue to destroy the environment.

⁂

When we walk into a big-box store, it's easy to feel defeated. Everything around us was either created with the intention to be a single-use, throwaway item or intentionally engi-neered to break so that we will have to buy it again—a tactic called "planned obsolescence." This is utter madness. Noth-ing the corporate goliaths try to sell you allows you to live in alignment with Mother Earth.

It's nearly impossible to live our lives without taking part in many of these malicious systems. This is a simple truth of the world as it is right now. It took hundreds of years for these evils to become so pervasive, and it's going to take some time to unravel them all. So, if a small amount of hypocrisy is the price, we must pay to end the tyranny of dirty fossil fuels, immoral food and farming practices, never-ending wars, and other harmful and destructive industries, then so be it. It is not inauthentic to do what you can and, at the same time, live in the world we have. Don't ever forget that the little, everyday decisions we make can change the world.

This life is a gift and it is our responsibility to respect and protect that which gives us life. . . . Every generation leaves a mark on this planet. We leave something behind to be remembered by, and we are at a tipping point right now where we will either be remembered as a generation that destroyed the planet, as a generation that put profits before future, or as a generation that united to address the greatest issue of our time by changing our relationship with the earth. We are being called upon to use our courage, our innovation, our creativity and our passion to bring forth a new world. So, in the light of this collapsing world that we see—what better time to be born than now? What better time to be alive than now? Because this generation . . . we get to change the course of history. Humans have created the greatest crisis that we see on the planet, and the greater the challenge, the higher we will rise to overcome it.

— Xiuhtezcatl Martinez, indigenous climate activist, address to the United Nations General Assembly on Climate Change, June 2015

The Way of the Seven Generations is about living in alignment with the ways of Grandmother Earth, and that must include taking action, regardless of our political beliefs. Doing what you can, when you can, with what you have, is always a good start. Taking responsibility is as simple as showing up and asking, "How can I be of service to Grandmother Earth today?" Growing a garden is a direct action. Getting debt-free is a direct action. Voting out weak and corrupt politicians is a direct action. Encouraging a friend going through a hard time is a direct action. Talking to a manager at a restaurant about getting rid of single-use plastic or foam take-out containers is a direct action. Refusing to take part in animal cruelty entertainment is a direct action. In fact, simply being happy is one of the most powerful forms of direct action you can take! Changed behavior, combined with consistent, everyday actions, compounded by many people, can change the world . . . and it's the only thing that ever has.

SPIRITUAL ACTIVATION: AKÍČHITA—EARTH WARRIOR

When at first you begin to take a stand and use your voice, it will be uncomfortable for everyone, including yourself. But, in a nonviolent struggle, our most powerful weapon is an army of like-minded people with a spark in their hearts born of the same sacred fire. Our enemies are powerful, and they may be able to blow out a single flame, but they cannot blow out a wildfire. When we rise up and bring direct action and awareness to an injustice, we're not saying and doing controversial things to make people unhappy or angry; we're saying and doing these things to get them uncomfortable with their privilege and apathy. We're not protesting, we're *protecting*, and by taking nonviolent, direct action, we're not fighting with our enemies. In essence, we're praying for them.

> *I sincerely encourage each one of you to take it upon*
> *yourself to become a warrior of one. Educate yourself.*
> *Find the knowledge it takes to survive and thrive in a*
> *good way. And to confront the ignorance of those who*
> *are destroying the natural. Confront them in such a way*
> *that they will come to know that to destroy the earth,*
> *to destroy our people, to continually ignore a philosophy*
> *and teachings that allowed this land to exist since the*
> *beginning of time in a beautiful natural existence, they*
> *will ultimately destroy themselves and all life.*
>
> — LEONARD PELTIER, FREEDOM FIGHTER AND POLITICAL
> PRISONER OF THE U.S. GOVERNMENT

Any direct action you take for the betterment of Grandmother Earth makes you an earth warrior. True warriors do not invade or occupy other countries to destabilize their governments and exploit the land on behalf of corrupt politicians and their greedy corporate sponsors. People who do this aren't warriors, they're just oppression-for-hire soldiers. The difference being that a soldier is told what to do, but a warrior already knows what to do, because they've been raised to care for the people and the land. Genuine warriors do not take; they give. They don't destroy; they build. They don't abuse; they nurture. They don't hurt; they heal. They don't murder; they hold space for all life. To be a warrior is to be in service to the family, the community, and to Grandmother Earth. A warrior is willing to sacrifice all to protect the well-being of self and others by confronting the enemy. A spiritual warrior fights not because they hate the person in front of them but because they love the people behind them. It is no longer acceptable to just toe the line of injustice; we must activate and step over that line. We must warrior up, get to the front lines, and take direct action.

When you are in direct action as a warrior—when you're facing the enemy—there will come a moment when your courage will end and fear will begin, when fear will now be in control of the situation. But then, often, something extraordinary will happen. A warrior, a spirit horse, will rise within you, surging forward. On its back will be courage—and not that first level of courage that got you to this point. This type of courage is a whole other level of energy. It is something that is truer, more sacred, and more powerful. This level of courage delivers you the clarity to see beyond the illusions of the world we live in today. This level of courage is impenetrable and indestructible. For those of you that will get that far, in that moment you will experience true freedom and there's nothing else like it in the world. Just ask anyone who took action against the Nazis in the 1940s, who battled against apartheid in South Africa for over three decades, or who challenged racism as a Freedom Rider in the 1960s. Ask the Water Protectors on the front lines at Standing Rock in 2016 or on the front lines protecting innocent black people from police brutality and murders in the nationwide riots of 2020. These warriors knew that doing the right thing could mean losing everything, but they're now forever painted with that next level of courage. Placing yourself on the front lines and squaring off face-to-face against injustice will change you forever.

Take that courage and be fearless. Even though we may take direct action against an injustice, it doesn't mean we're fighting. It simply means that we've put our prayer into action. We must never be in a position to have to apologize to the children of the future that we sat idly by as spiritually disconnected humans set the world on fire for political agendas or corporate profits. The future seven generations will sing songs about how we fought for them with our presence and our prayers. When all seems hopeless, then there is truly nothing left to fear.

THE WAY OF THE BUFFALO

The Buffalo Nation and the Original Nations of Turtle Island are destined to share the same fate. When the Buffalo of the original ancient bloodline return and spread across the land, so will the beauty, abundance, and powerful healing of the old ways.

— DOUG GOOD FEATHER

The Way of the Buffalo is about our relationship with the abundant gifts our Grandmother Earth offers us every day.

This way of life teaches us that we take only what we need and that we use everything we take.

By her very nature, our beautiful Grandmother Earth is incredibly generous. Her abundance is ever present; it's everywhere and there is never a lack of it. When we feel limitations and obstacles to abundance, they are of our own human creation. When we find ourselves in a time of life when we're struggling or lacking something we desperately need, it's time to remember who we are and our place in this universe. Don't pray for abundance. Instead, pray for the obstacles that prevent you from seeing the abundance that's already all around you to be removed from your mind and heart. Abundance is something to sink into and allow.

The universe provides for us in incalculable ways. When we experience tough times, it is because we have forgotten that so much has been sacrificed for us to be here so we can truly *be* here. We deserve to be at peace, be satisfied, and be safe to float down the river of life's adventures. We are so blessed. We just need to remember how blessed we are and how those blessings came to be.

THE STORY OF THE BUFFALO PEOPLE

Deep in the heart of winter, during the moon when the trees crack from the cold and in a time before the White Buffalo Calf Woman, begins the story of a small family that was suffering from illness and starvation and facing imminent death. All seemed hopeless, so with her last remaining strands of consciousness, a young mother prayed deeply for the Creator to come and save her family. As this woman prayed, a great sleep overcame her and she awoke in her dream. She was standing in a meadow and a gold light drifted toward her through the waving grasses. A voice that was not her own reso- nated throughout her body and gave her a message. It was only a moment, but in that moment, she was told that her husband was to go to the highest ground he could find and pray for the Great Mystery to take pity on their family. Then she woke, bolting upright with a great gasp as this epiphany lit up her eyes. She told her husband of the message and what he was to do.

Although starving and clinging to life, the young husband left immediately. It was bone-numbing cold, but he made it to the highest ground he was able. He called out to the Creator to take pity on his family and help them to live. As the man prayed with every fiber of his being, a great snowstorm arose and swirled around him and he collapsed onto the icy ground. With his last bit of life force, the young father lifted his head just in time to see a brilliant ray of white light pierce through the storm. The man thought this was the Great Spirit coming to take him back home. But the light drew into itself and took the form of a giant buffalo.

The buffalo was majestic. He walked up to the man and contemplated him in a long silence before speaking. "Dear Brother, the Creator has heard your cries and has sent me to witness your suffering. As I look at you, I see you are not equipped to live in the ways of this land." The magnificent buffalo slowly circled the young man. "I see that you are freezing, yet I am warm. I see that you are weak, yet I am strong." The buffalo lowered his head closer to the young man. "I see your fingers are delicate and cannot dig for food, yet I paw the ground and the ice breaks effortlessly."

The buffalo raised his massive head and as his breath mixed with the winter air, he looked down the hill onto the vast prairie below. "You are sure to perish, having that body and trying to live on this land." The mighty buffalo turned back to the man. "Brother, I feel your suffering and I understand your desire to live, so listen carefully to my words." As the buffalo spoke, the storm began to break, and the blue sky could be seen through the clouds. "I will make you this sacred promise that will bond our two nations all the rest of our days. You and I are now connected beyond the ways of flesh and bone and related in all the ways known to the Creator."

The buffalo lowered his massive head, connecting forehead-to-forehead with the man, in which position they shared each other's breath. "I will help your family and all the families that will come onto this land after you, until the end of time. I will give you my hide so that you may warm yourself. I will give you my flesh so that you may feed yourself. I will give you my bones so that you may make tools and weapons to dig with and defend yourself. Watch what we eat, so that you may know what to eat for nourishment and medicine. Watch how we travel these lands, how we raise our children, and how we live as a community, so that your two-legged nation may learn how to thrive and treat one another with dignity. Our people will show you the ways of living with Grandmother Earth."

The buffalo motioned with his head for the man to get up. "I make this promise on behalf of all my people of the Great Buffalo Nation, but you must only take what you need and use everything you take and after you have received the blessing of our bond, you must give thanks to the Creator for this Sacred Hoop of Life." The man rose up and followed the buffalo down the hill, onto the prairie, and back to his family with the gift and promise of the Buffalo People. And it was so, and so it is to this day.

HÁU, MITÁKUYE OYÁS'IŊ

To the indigenous nomadic tribes of the Northern Plains, the Pté Oyáte—the Buffalo People—buffalo provide more than just clothing, food, tools, spiritual ceremony, medicine, and shelter for the people. They are also honored relatives, with no point of distinction between where the life force of the buffalo ends and the human's begins.

The buffalo taught the indigenous people of the original nations how to nurture and protect one another. When the buffalo are under attack, they go into warrior mode and form an outward-facing circle. The strongest warriors in the herd are on the outer ring, and the elders, the young, and those unable to defend themselves are protected inside of the circle. It is a living, breathing barrier of massive primordial strength and horns. A single upward thrust from a bull buffalo can launch a full-grown wolf 30 feet in the air. When they're traveling and there's a weak or injured buffalo in the herd, a group of other buffalo will travel along with it so it doesn't feel vulnerable and lonely. There are many buffalo teachings that we can integrate into our human ways, and one of those lessons is to be mindful of the cause and effect of our daily actions. Never leave a warrior behind.

Mindful Consumption

Mindful Consumption is the modern way of thinking about the indigenous concept of taking only what we need and using everything we take. It's being intentional and deliberate, with full understanding that what we do and how we do it will impact our Mother Earth. To Think Indigenous is to be mindful and take complete responsibility for our personal consumerism and consumption.

This responsibility begins with each of us learning about the things we consume. Many of us have little to no idea about the sobering details of how our food or material goods get to us, where they come from, how they're grown or manufactured, where it all goes when we're done with it—and who and what's behind it all. In fact, what we consider garbage or trash is a modern invention that has manifested as a result of spiritually disconnected people walking away from their relationship with Grandmother Earth.

In the past, indigenous people lived with a circular mindset that everything they harvested or made was done with great consideration and intention, from the mere thought of its creation to its end of use, state of rest, or regeneration. Today, the global supply chain of food and material goods operates with a linear mindset, meaning there is zero consideration for their product after it's been sold to us. It's an act of extreme negligence for a company to produce a product with no comprehensive plan for its end-of-use life.

In fact, many corporations go beyond deliberately ignoring what happens to their products at the end of usability, actually engineering failure and obsolescence into their products. Corporations intentionally do this, so their products prematurely wear out or break in order to force replacement and the corporations maintain their long-term sales. Having a zero-waste mindset isn't about producing or consuming nothing; it's about carefully and intentionally designing, producing, and consuming without waste as an end result.

As a society, when we see corporations and executives practicing planned obsolescence with their products, it is best to help them set better intentions and practices through our choices regarding what we buy and accept as a product or service we actually use. When we see a company operating with intention, high quality, and a collective consciousness for its role in the supply chain of the world's food or material goods, we need to recognize and support its efforts. Our choosing to praise and support good effort encourages an immediate redirect of bad corporate practices.

We can start by not buying toxic food and trying to buy only naturally grown food that comes from local farmers. If your local grocery store doesn't have an ample supply of this type of food, then request it. Vendors will supply what consumers ask for. People inform companies how to behave and create based on their spending. Being informed and educating yourself to understand which companies support things you don't believe in will guide you on how and where to spend your money and cast your vote. The items you purchase, what you watch, and what you read all contribute to your mindful consumption.

Our Trash Tells a Story
If our trash could tell us its story, it would be a story about what humans value—or, rather, what we *don't* value.

But imagine if we all made less trash. Imagine if we embodied more resourcefulness, thriftiness, and community focus. Imagine if we gave companies and manufacturers a reason to change their packaging and recover their materials after a product's life.

Each of us can make dramatically less waste. Each of us can reconsider what we consume. Even the simple act of refusing a plastic straw at a restaurant or bringing your own cup to a coffee shop makes a difference. And, of great importance, we must refuse any and all single-use plastics. What will we use instead? Hemp. Hemp is Grandmother Earth's perfect plant. Hemp is natural, not synthetic, and can heal our addiction to petroleum and other harmful and inferior products. We can all support hemp as a source material for products, food, fuel, fiber, medicine, and construction materials. The liberation of hemp is the tip of the spear in the battles being waged by many humanitarian and environmental movements. As consumers, we can all encourage the farmers of the world to grow hemp as part of our mindful consumption.

Are these small efforts simply doing too little, too late? No! Little actions lead to big changes, and we never know whom we are going to inspire that will rise and lead their own homegrown (r)evolution against one or more of the many injustices we face as a unified family.

SPIRITUAL ACTIVATION: MAKȞÁ WÓWAŠ'AKE—EARTH ENERGY

Every sentient being on earth has a life force and every life force has a period of time in which it is active and a period of time in which it is at rest. Circling this Sacred Hoop of Life is part of the journey for all beings. There's a reason that we don't disturb the life force of a being when its spirit has passed over and its remains are in a state of rest. It's an inherent understanding that it's the worst kind of bad medicine to dig up our relatives from their graves. When we disrupt the natural harmony of Grandmother Earth by digging up her remains—her oil, gas, and ore—we create imbalance, which will eventually manifest as suffering, disease, death, and destruction.

We are all passive addicts of the petroleum industry and we have to accept responsibility for that fact. Collectively, we must lead the transition of our energy needs away from dirty fossil fuels toward renewable and regenerative energy sources. The biggest threat to our planet is apathy. Many people assume that some group of scientists must surely be working day and night in some secret lab to save the planet. Let's get real. No one is going to save us from ourselves. There is no "someone else" taking care of our trash and climate crisis. We are the ones we've been waiting for, and only we can do something about it.

Natural elements are not just waiting around for humans to come and extract them—in such destructive ways—as profitable resources; these elements serve other functions for Grandmother Earth. When humans are detached from the ways of the Mother, they carry out all sorts of ignorant atrocities, such as when humans think it's a good idea to build dams or divert water to control or cut off life-giving channels of energy. So much suffering comes as a result of ignorant humans trying to control the energy of sacred water.

Stop and think about it for a moment. Stopping the migration routes of our salmon relatives creates cascading instances of imbalance and suffering across multiple ecosystems. We must work with the energy of our natural elements, not against those energies. A dam is not the only solution to harness the power of water. If there is not a source of water for a city on a particular piece of land, then we should not build a city there. If there is a sacred mountain that no human should build upon, then we should not build there. These are uncomplicated concepts made complicated by humans who have no understanding of the spirit of the land.

Spiritual intelligence tells us that we don't need to extract harmful fossil fuels for our energy. All we have to do is look to the indigenous ways of thinking about living in a good way, the Sacred Hoop of Life, the medicine wheel, the ways of medicine and spirit, and the four sacred directions to find solutions.

So, where do we get unlimited renewable energy?

EAST: Solar Power—The Sun
SOUTH: Wind Power—The Air
WEST: Water Power—The Water
NORTH: Geothermal and Biofuels—The Earth

We've now learned so many ways to help bring harmony and balance back to the ways of the spirit of Grandmother Earth. She gives us abundance and we must receive it responsibly. The easiest way to do so is to apply kindness, care, awareness, and spiritual intelligence to every choice we make, including our basic, everyday activities.

The Journey from a Linear Mindset to a Circular Mindset
A linear mindset consists of thinking of getting from Point A (product) to Point B (profit). A circular mindset requires

taking that process several steps further, until you come all the way back around to the beginning. Point A to point B, and then what? What happens with all the trash we've created? What happens when we create things with the intention that they will become obsolete? What is at the end of the line of that linear thought? The answers to seemingly difficult questions become clear when we Think Indigenous.

A circular mindset mirrors the essence of nature's systems in relation to our food and material goods. It supports the health and well-being of the communities we live in, how we grow the food we eat, how we support the people who create what we use, and how we manage our spiritual relationship with the source of the material used from our Grandmother Earth. It's a mindset and lifestyle respectful and reflective of how the earth creates, uses, nurtures, recovers, and balances her interconnected natural systems.

This circular "medicine wheel" mindset is also about bringing awareness to an ignored conversation about our misuse of resources, the environmental impact our throwaway culture has created on the planet, and how we can simplify our wants and needs to bring value back to our communities. It's about starting conversations about mindful consumption, inspiring each other, and living by example in the middle of our current throwaway culture. Each one of us can take ownership of the power we have and intentionally make less waste. When we do, we feel the satisfying emotional effects of slowing down, simplifying our busy lives, and putting meaning and value back into our belongings, communities, and environment.

There's a common saying that if we want to change the world, then we need to be that change. It's so simple, and yet it embodies a clear message that our lifestyles, habits, and actions are the foundation of creating this change.

Nothing has ever happened on its own without the individual consistent dedication of many people acting on their convictions.
The world we desire—which I imagine would be peaceful, tolerant, compassionate, balanced, and wise— won't exist unless we become what we want to see.

— ANDREA SANDERS, FOUNDER OF THE
BIOMINDFULNESS MOVEMENT

In order to make this change, we need to do the work. We have to open ourselves up to something new, separate ourselves from the noise, labels, and boxes in order to do something bigger than ourselves. The way to live in a circular mindset is to mimic nature, which is a notion of living with the natural systems of the earth. It begins with a sense of value, community, responsibility, ownership, and simplicity that weaves through our lives and creates the fabric of our communities and culture.

Being mindful of our consumption is not about achieving some level of zero-waste perfection, nor is it only some more stuff for us to do in our already busy lives. Mindful consumption is our way of being in a committed relationship with ourselves and Grandmother Earth.

THE WAY OF THE VILLAGE

You want to be tough?
You want to be a warrior?
You want to be invincible?
Then show the whole world your heart.

— DOUG GOOD FEATHER

Indigenous cultures strive to identify and honor each person's unique identity. They collectively support each person's distinct value and contribution to the community. This comes from the mindset that everyone is important because everyone is a teacher. We need to encourage others to find their calling and the role they are most inclined to do. We must not judge anyone, because we have no idea what storm the Creator asked that person to walk through. However, holding someone responsible for deliberately compromising their morals is not judging them; it's holding them accountable to their role and behavior in the unified family.

It can be frustrating trying to find a community that fits who we are, let alone what role we serve. Unfortunately, the ways of the modern world encourage us to envy each other. If somebody is better at something than we are, we might envy them a bit, but what we have to remember is that they are not naturally endowed with that skill or talent. They had to work hard to perfect the skill and practice to become an expert. If you envy someone else's ability to paint or sing, then that is setting aside your own natural skills and talents. The answer is not to compete and force yourself into a role that is unnatural for you. Instead, find your passion, what you are naturally inclined to do, and practice that skill until you become an expert. Your role will be upheld and revered as much as everyone else's.

Culture is when people in a community share a belief system of values and objectives, and it's where we collaborate in a way that's for the best and highest good of the community.

Collective Impact

Collective Impact is the ancestral knowing that there is strength in numbers. A proverb from the indigenous peoples says one single willow branch is weak but the strength of many willows is unbreakable. We can accomplish nearly anything when we put our hearts and minds together.

Find Your Community
When we begin to Think Indigenous and our relationship with spirituality continues to grow, each new level of understanding and self-awareness will create a new version of ourselves. We need to be aware that our new spiritual understandings and realizations may cause a deep dissatisfaction with and resentment of our current employment situation, personal behaviors, lifestyle, or living conditions. As we spiritually evolve, our relationships with friends, family, co-workers, and our partner or spouse will change as well. With new mindsets, certain people who are close to you might have a difficult time understanding the changes you are making. When you are confident enough to love yourself and start doing what's best for you, it will change your life for the better, but not everyone will understand this since it is a new action for you. As we know every action has a reaction and not everyone will appreciate the changes. We need to take a moment to honor ourselves and think about how long we've been on our personal spiritual journey, working on our self-awareness, improving ourselves, and working on our relationship to this life and this world. The loss of a relationship is of little consequence in comparison with the loss of our spirit.

We must keep in mind that though we are expanding our spiritual consciousness and personal awareness, we cannot force others to resonate with knowledge that they are not yet ready to receive. In fact, an indigenous proverb tells us that it's useless to speak butterfly language to caterpillar people. It may be difficult to continue a personal connection with the many people in our lives who have not experienced the level of profound personal awareness and deep spiritual connection with the Great Spirit that we are experiencing. It's important to keep in mind that someone can only connect with you as deeply as they've connected with themselves. From time to time we will simply evolve beyond certain people and the Creator will take us in a different direction in life. This is part of our awakening.

But in this awakening, as we begin to lose connection with certain people, circumstances, and things in our conventional lives, it's common to become frustrated or feel isolated and lonely. For this reason, it's important that we search for people on a similar journey to our own. We need to identify our community of like-minded individuals and seek their spiritual support, teachings, and practices so that we can continue to move forward with our connection with Spirit, our spiritual self-actualization, and our passion and purpose in service to Grandmother Earth.

Home Is a Feeling

Scandinavia is made up of several Nordic countries in northern Europe, and the indigenous people of that region have a rich culture. Their ancient practice of paganism reaches back into some of the oldest recorded spiritual history known to humankind. The people of the Nordic countries experience some of the most challenging winter conditions on the planet. There's barely any sunlight to break up the monotony of their long, cold winters—however, there's also a mystical beauty when the land settles into its deep slumber of winter.

The people who make their homes here have found a way to find joy and comfort even in conditions that those who live further south would find unbearable. What they understand is that home is not so much a place as it is a *feeling*. The Danes and the Norwegians have a word that evokes that enigmatic feeling of home: *hygge* (pronounced "hoo-guh"). Hygge doesn't translate into a definable word in any other language, but it is essentially a combination of comfort, coziness, nurturing, kinship, contentment, and simplicity. Hygge is the art of creating intimacy in our sacred places, including our home and community.

Hygge isn't a particular lifestyle, nor is it something that can be bought—it is the act of thoughtfully shaping your way of life into an art form. Hygge is the simple joy of a home-cooked meal with friends around the table, or taking the time for a cup of mint tea in front of a fire, or snuggling up with a loved one and talking about the good things in life. It's living life intentionally and honoring the little things that make memories and life worth living.

Hygge is healing. In order to be effective in the world and in our communities, we have to make sure we ourselves are working on our healing before we try to help or heal others. As I say, in order to heal the land, we must heal each other, but to heal each other, we must first heal our self. Creating a feeling of comfort, security, health, and intimacy in our homes and community may be more necessary now than ever.

Life with a Healing Community

To be a valued family member of a community, we have to put down the modern-world mantra of "What's in it for me?" and put ourselves in the headspace and heart space of collective well-being. A member of the community should have a strong sense of self-identity without being self-absorbed, self-centered, or self-serving.

It is good to grow deep roots within our community and that means that we must go deep into ourselves and deep into our commitment to being on a spiritual path.

We don't need to be related by blood or through marriage to be a family. Being a family simply means that we share a common purpose and that we're devoted to a common mission. The Lakota have the word *thiyóšpaye*, which refers to our extended family. A family holds space for one another with unconditional love and understanding. We protect one another; we pick up where the other leaves off, and we are strong for one another when someone may be weak.

We are human, so sometimes we want to control people with conditions on our love, and sometimes our understanding is not so understanding. But those times are our opportunities to help bring our family back to the true meaning of "unconditional" and "understanding." We're not meant to be perfect—but we are meant to keep trying and to keep loving unconditionally. Of course, "unconditional" does not mean the absence of healthy boundaries. Becoming a family takes time, so be patient with yourself and one another by honoring the process of being a family.

Holding Space
Holding space means to be deliberately present in emotional and energetic support of something or someone, as when a spiritual teacher holds space for us to remember what we have forgotten but have always known. However, we don't need to be a spiritual teacher to hold space to help one another. We can hold space by actively listening and observing without judgment as a filter, by acting in such a way that whoever we're holding space for knows that we're right there with them, even if we're a thousand miles away. All over the world, there are people being held as political prisoners and we have warriors holding up the front line, defending Grandmother Earth against governments and corporations. Closer to home, we may have a family member who is succumbing to the effects of cancer and chemotherapy in a hospital, or a friend that's grieving or going through a relationship breakup. These are the people we hold space for.

To be effective when we hold space, it cannot just be once or twice, or something that's done sporadically—it has to be done consistently. Our ability to hold space and simply *be there* in solidarity may often be more helpful than anything we could think to say or do to support each other in difficult times.

Community is made up of two words: communication and unity. We heal ourselves by honoring each other.

SPIRITUAL ACTIVATION: ÁYA IGLÚHA—BECOMING SOVEREIGN

With regard to living according to the Way of the Community, there are two meanings to the word *sovereign*. In order to be a true, contributing part of your community, *you* must be sovereign within that community, meaning you must be self-reliant and reliable. Think about when you've passed someone struggling to move a couch into their apartment or a mother struggling to get her stroller up the stairs or through a door. Jumping in to help is how to be a part of a community, even if these are people you will never see again. And making sure that when it's your turn to move a couch, you've arranged enough friends, so you don't *need* unplanned help is how you carry your own weight within that community. Each of us must show up on our own, in our own way, in order to be a true part of the whole. Each of us is equally important. The Hawaiian term for this is *kuleana*, which loosely translates to "responsibility": you have a responsibility to help others, but also to help yourself.

We are built to be in a community. And it's our human nature to get lonely; we need the companionship of others. But it can be difficult to find your people. So often, we not only don't help out with couch-moving, we even pretend not to recognize our neighbors when we pass them on the street. Much too often, we refuse to acknowledge the existence of those we feel can do nothing for us. We must break out of this conditioning and make the effort to engage with others even though they may pretend not to notice us. The world is a better place with communities of like-minded people doing good things in the world.

The people around you are your community. The people who live on the same floor in your apartment building, or the neighbors in your cul-de-sac, or the people who all work in the same office space—your community is not just your friends or family, it's everyone you exist with in your concentric circle of community.

And when we find our community, we can then work on becoming sovereign by living, working, and playing with that same circular mindset. My neighbor has bell peppers and I have eggs. The teenager across the street can help the auntie down the block figure out how to video chat with her grandchildren and she can pick up her neighbor's kids from school when he has to work late. We are stronger together than we are apart—we are sovereign together and we are self-sustaining together. That is the way of the community.

THE WAY FORWARD

Now that you've come this far on the path of these teachings, what is your "aha!" moment? What has struck you deeply, has made you want to be bold with where you go from here? To live happier, stronger, more connected, more empowered? What are you never going to forget? When we share something, when we talk about it, when we actually do it, that's what makes it real. Right now, come tell us about it:

www.LakotaWay.org

Each time we accept a new perspective on ourselves, we grow. Where did you grow? How are you different? What did you learn that grew your awareness? We truly want to know so that we can support you on your journey—and learn from you as we continue on ours. For we are all teachers, and we all learn from one another.

Life is not meant to be easy—it's meant to teach you. There will always be moments and people who challenge you, who bring trouble into your life. These people and these moments are showing up in your life as teachers. What is this challenge trying to teach you?

Once you recognize that your moments are teachers, it's much easier to overcome hardship. Use the methods and tools we've shared to overcome these challenges and troubles and learn what they are trying to teach you, incorporating it into your knowledge and understanding of how to live.

Our wish is for you to continue the journey. To take what you have learned and bring these ways of thinking into your everyday life.

How? First, it starts from within. Make the decision and dedicate yourself to it.

Second, find something to stand for and warrior up. What have you witnessed that you know is harmful or destructive? Examine that and take it into your life. Retell the story, live it, activate it. *Being a spiritual warrior is a way of life.*

Third, find your community. Reach out to those around you, build bridges, and find the people who will support you in your growth and who will grow with you.

We're one people; we're one nation; we're all indigenous to Mother Earth. And making life more beautiful is going to take all of us.

With love,
Doug Good Feather

HÁU, MITÁKUYE OYÁS'IŊ

ACKNOWLEDGMENTS

First, I humbly acknowledge the Creator and Mother Earth for giving me this life and hardships; without both this book would have never been possible.

I would like to express my special thanks of gratitude to my elders who showed me these ways; they showed me these ways are real. They instilled in me everything I teach and everything I have learned, whether it is spiritual or scientific. Felix Kills Pretty Enemy and Noah Has Horns gave me their time, patience, teachings, and unconditional love. I am overwhelmed in all humbleness and gratefulness to acknowledge my deep and sincere gratitude to them for my foundation in this world.

I also would like to humbly acknowledge and give my everlasting gratitude for Oley Little Eagle and Madeline Kills Pretty Enemy Little Eagle for teaching me the laws of nature, to sing and work hard. They raised me in the old ways to work hard and be honest in all I do. Madeline was the matriarch of our family and taught all of us the traditional ways of our people. She was strong and wise and showed me how to respect women as the head of the home and backbone of the people. Oley was an amazing father, composer, and fluent Lakota speaker, and he taught me our traditional songs. Every time I return home, my first stop is to visit with him, and he would always greet me with a welcome home song. We would sing together, and I will remember him every time I sing for the rest of my life. I miss them dearly, but I know they gave me the gift of our traditional ways and language for our people will live on forever.

To Doug Red Hail Pineda, Amy Star Speaker, and all those who have helped me to put these ideas well above the level of simplicity in my mind into something concrete, I am grateful and humbled by your dedication to hearing these teachings to help make this book a reality. Thank you.

—Doug Good Feather

My mother, Lucy Pineda, taught me that one of the highest forms of intelligence is the ability to question what I know to be true. I am truly humbled and grateful for her wisdom. My father, Dan Pineda, was the seventh son of a seventh son and by far the most authentic and truthful human I have ever known. I am deeply honored to be his son and so thankful to witness someone whose words actually matched their actions. The lessons my parents taught me about truth is what set me on my spiritual path and gave me the ability to help create this book. Seeking truth will humble you in many unexpected ways. I wish you all a clear path and a good journey as you seek your truth.

Mitákuye Oyás'iŋ

—Doug Red Hail Pineda

ABOUT THE AUTHOR

Doug Good Feather is a full-blooded native American Lakota, born and raised in the traditional indigenous ways of his elders on the Standing Rock Indian Reservation in South Dakota. He is a direct descendant of Grandpa Chief Sitting Bull. He is the executive director and spiritual leader of the Lakota Way in Colorado and the co-founder of Spirit Horse Nation. You can visit Lakota Way Healing Center online at Lakotaway.org.

Hay House Titles of Related Interest

We hope you enjoyed this Hay House book. If you'd like to receive our online catalog featuring additional information on Hay House books and products, or if you'd like to find out more about the Hay Foundation, please contact:

Hay House, Inc., P.O. Box 5100, Carlsbad, CA 92018-5100
(760) 431-7695 or (800) 654-5126
(760) 431-6948 (fax) or (800) 650-5115 (fax)
www.hayhouse.com® • www.hayfoundation.org

———

Published in Australia by: Hay House Australia Pty. Ltd.,
18/36 Ralph St., Alexandria NSW 2015
Phone: 612-9669-4299 • *Fax:* 612-9669-4144
www.hayhouse.com.au

Published in the United Kingdom by: Hay House UK, Ltd.,
The Sixth Floor, Watson House, 54 Baker Street, London W1U 7BU
Phone: +44 (0)20 3927 7290 • *Fax:* +44 (0)20 3927 7291
www.hayhouse.co.uk

Published in India by: Hay House Publishers India,
Muskaan Complex, Plot No. 3, B-2, Vasant Kunj, New Delhi 110 070
Phone: 91-11-4176-1620 • *Fax:* 91-11-4176-1630
www.hayhouse.co.in

———

Access New Knowledge.
Anytime. Anywhere.

Learn and evolve at your own pace
with the world's leading experts.

www.hayhouseU.com